SOCIOLOGY AND SOCIAL WELFARE SERIES

edited by Paul Halmos

Without a Wedding-Ring

IN THE SAME SERIES

Social Science and Social Purpose
T. S. Simey

Industrial Democracy: The Sociology of Participation
Paul Blumberg

Without a Wedding-Ring

CASEWORK WITH UNMARRIED PARENTS

Jean Pochin

with a foreword by
Pauline Shapiro

Schocken Books · New York

Published in U.S.A. in 1969
by Schocken Books Inc.
67 Park Avenue, New York, N.Y. 10016

Library of Congress Catalog Card No. 72–84196
Printed in Great Britain

For Herbert and Celia Batey

Foreword

Without a Wedding-Ring appears opportunely, since remarkably little has been written in this country about social casework with unmarried parents. The lack of published material is the more surprising in view of the rise in the rate of illegitimacy and the concern it is causing. Books that have appeared recently about unmarried mothers have been more concerned to ask who these are and why, rather than to discuss how best to offer help once pregnancy has occurred. It is true that effective help must begin with answers to such questions, and Miss Pochin considers these in the early chapters of her book. But she then proceeds to the practical and urgent question of what help should be offered in tackling this growing social problem. Now that punitive attitudes to unwed mothers are less widespread, it is easier to elicit understanding of the needs of a defenceless woman facing such a crucial experience as pregnancy without the support and sustaining interest of a husband. Each unwed mother has to make a grave decision, whether to keep her baby and fight against heavy odds or to struggle against her own instincts and surrender her child for adoption. How often is the right decision reached? Do social workers offer help in assessing such situations and what is the quality of that help? It may well be significant that in the United States 75 per cent of all illegitimate children are offered for adoption, whereas in this country the percentage is only 25. Yet we know nothing of the factors responsible for this difference. Moreover, we know very little about the fate of those children not offered for adoption. To some extent our lack of knowledge can be explained because a great number and variety of agencies are concerned with helping unmarried mothers and also with adoption, but at different stages and for varying lengths of time.

Miss Pochin had the inestimable advantage of working with unmarried mothers not only during their period of pregnancy and childbirth but also during the years that followed, whether the children were adopted or remained with mother, or with relatives. The rural nature of the area in which she worked helped her to maintain these contacts, and she was thus in a better position than social workers in many other agencies to give continuous help and gain a full understanding of the problems and how they may be resolved. During the sabbatical year she spent in the Social Administration Department of Birmingham University it quickly became clear that Miss Pochin possessed, as well as humanity and a sense of humour, extensive social work experience and a gift for writing. It seemed to us that this rare combination of gifts could contribute something exceptionally valuable to casework studies. We encouraged Miss Pochin, therefore, to extend her time with us in order to write about her casework experience. Thanks also to the support and interest of the Diocesan Council for Social Work she had an opportunity, such as is seldom available to busy social workers, to write this book.

Without a Wedding-Ring depicts vividly the plight of unmarried mothers, what their motives and misfortunes may have been and how social workers may offer help. It shows, also, how much we still need to learn about unmarried parents, particularly the fathers. Its discussion of relevant social provisions and the ways in which they might be improved is not only well informed but also timely. Its comprehensive survey will prove invaluable to all students of social work, not merely to those working and researching in this particular field. It is to be hoped that it will be widely read, for no contemporary social problem is more in need of informed consideration. Miss Pochin's book is clearly written, free from jargon, and amply illustrated with case examples; everyone, whether specialist or layman, will find it as readable as it is instructive.

Pauline Shapiro

Department of Social Administration
University of Birmingham

Preface

This book is based upon thirteen years of casework with unmarried mothers, unmarried fathers and their children. The community in which I worked was somewhat isolated geographically, and fortunate in having no colour problem and a reasonably high level of employment. Family ties were strong, and most of the single girls lived with their parents or other relatives.

Elsewhere, conditions may be very different; in certain city areas, for example, almost all the unmarried women will be lodging in bed-sitters or flatlets, at a distance from their homes. Hence the setting of the pregnant girl's problem varies greatly according to circumstances. The social provisions available also show great diversity in different parts of the country. In one place there may be no more than a single Mother and Baby Home and the basic allowances of the Ministry of Social Security. In big towns there tends to be a sort of factory process into which pregnant girls are 'fed' at one end, so that at the other there emerges an adopted baby and a 'normal' single girl, who has been transitorily in touch with perhaps a dozen different helpers in the meantime. A third area may be better provided with a skilled and continuous casework service, helpful voluntary organisations and available accommodation for single girls and their babies.

Naturally, I have said little about the many unmarried mothers who manage for themselves and have no contact with any casework agency. A large proportion of these live in stable cohabitation with the fathers of their children, and others in communities where illegitimate children are accepted without difficulty. But the problems of unmarried parenthood remain basically the same in our society whatever the circumstances, and it is mostly upon the common ground that I have trodden in this book.

With regard to the case material, fictitious names have been used and circumstantial details altered to prevent the identification of individuals, without altering the basic situation.

I am most sincerely grateful to the Board for Social Responsibility of the Church Assembly, the Queen's College at Birmingham and the Faculty of Social Studies of Birmingham University, who have made it possible for me to review the case records of some seven hundred illegitimate pregnancies in the light of what has already been written, and the research studies of unmarried parenthood which have been made, both in this country and in the United States. In particular I am happy to acknowledge my debt to Mrs P. C. Shapiro of Birmingham University, who first suggested that I should write this book, and who has helped and encouraged me at every step.

I must express my thanks also to the Chairman and Committee of the casework agency concerned for their permission to use the case material, to the clients themselves, to Mrs E. Winfield who typed so efficiently from a chaotic manuscript, and to many friends for their comments and criticism. 'Model Love Song' by Peter Dickinson is reprinted by permission of *Punch*.

Contents

1. The Unmarried Mother

Who is she?

Carol was as glamorous as a television starlet, charming, ingenuous, irresponsible. 'You know,' she said as she travelled towards the Mother and Baby Home, 'I used to think it was only *common* girls who had babies.'

This is one pregnant girl's view of unmarried motherhood. Few people arouse more confused reactions in society than the single girl who gives birth to a child, and everyone has his own ideas about her identity and character. It is only a century since 'fallen women' were separated sharply by public opinion from the rest of fallen mankind, and a lot of the old ambivalence still lingers. 'She's no better than she should be' is a common way of describing a woman with a pram but no wedding-ring. Such a woman makes her neighbours feel uncomfortable, perhaps because she touches upon their own profound sensitivities with regard to sexuality. Deep down, they may recognise impulses to the same kind of behaviour in themselves, and so they may envy her because she seems to be less inhibited than they, and has actually got her baby. Or they may simply feel guilty and then their instinctive reaction is hatred, fear and rejection. Yet there is an element of compassion, too, which constrains most people to be nice to the girl herself whatever they may feel about her conduct. This confusion is typical of our society as a whole, and will not be easily resolved because it reflects the tension always present between instinct and the moral law. In some sections of the community, naturally, sympathy is predominant, and elsewhere criticism; the attitude of individuals and special groups varies from the abruptly condemning 'I've no patience – it's a sin', through indifference to the frankly lustful. Ignorance has worsened the emotional muddle, and understanding based on knowledge is still too rare.

It is only recently that any clear distinction has been made between the professional prostitute, who makes her living by the use of her body but seldom becomes pregnant, and the girl who bears a child for totally different reasons. Prostitutes have long been outcasts from society, and any unmarried girl who had a baby was, until the beginning of this century, most often dismissed without further enquiry as a 'harlot' or 'loose woman'. Was not the child the proof of her immorality? Out with her, then. After Moll Flanders, the penitent prostitute became a stock figure of sentimentality in countless novels and plays, and the Victorians who shed tears over her were equally sentimental over the luckless girl who was 'betrayed' by her lover, but they hardly distinguished between the two. The pregnant unmarried woman still had to suffer the full social penalties. Indeed, it was that that was so heartrendingly sad about her – that her cruel father drove her out into the snow, friendless and penniless – not her gullibility or her hunger for love. Hardly anyone enquired how it happened, or cared very much, although some enlightened people in every age have been concerned to show mercy to the 'fallen sisterhood'. One of these was Thomas Coram of the Foundling Hospital, who was deeply distressed by 'the morbid morality possessing the public mind by which the unhappy female who fell a victim to the seductions and false promises of designing men' was condemned to 'hopeless contumely and irretrievable disgrace'.[1*] A hundred years later, Josephine Butler and her associates drove home the point that there would be no immoral women if there were no immoral men. She found ample proof that in the social conditions of her time it was this general ostracism of the unmarried mother, together with the restricted opportunities then open for women to earn their own living, that drove many girls to prostitution.

The wave of concern for the moral welfare of the nation that Josephine Butler set in motion produced a multitude of theories about the causes of illegitimate pregnancy, many of which were partly correct, but it was not until scientific methods began to be applied to the study of human behaviour, and in particular as the implications of Freud's work became known and accepted, that any real understanding began to be possible. It is largely owing to psychology that society's attitude towards its deviants has in general become kinder and wiser. We have insight into hidden motives and unconscious drives that was not available to our grandparents, and this has produced in us a more realistic compassion. The common saying that 'it isn't the girls who *have* babies who are immoral, it's the ones who *don't*' shows at least

* Notes and references begin on p. 153.

that the distinction between the unmarried mother and the prostitute has at last penetrated the public consciousness. The blanket of condemnation is being lifted from both. It is interesting to compare Nathaniel Hawthorne's attitude of indignant pity, considerably mixed with revulsion and patronage, towards Hester Prynne, who is the unmarried mother heroine of *The Scarlet Letter*, a novel he finished in 1850, with the tender objectivity of Dylan Thomas's treatment of Polly Garter, the prostitute in *Under Milk Wood*. We now see unmarried pregnancy not as a deadly sin, but as a grave symptom.

Another, more disturbing reason for the change of view is that unmarried motherhood has come home to us all, and lives now in our street. Condemnation has given place to a fear that after all it could happen in our family. Carol was indeed mistaken in her idea that it is only 'common' girls who have babies; a caseworker looking through her files will find a bank manager's fourteen-year-old daughter listed next to a factory girl aged nineteen, and followed perhaps by a woman of thirty who helps her brother to run a shop. Unmarried pregnancy certainly knows no bounds of age, social class or intelligence. In Great Britain the problem of schoolgirl mothers is no longer news, and we have a number of Mother and Baby Homes where morning lessons are the rule. It is interesting, therefore, to find that in America during the early 'sixties 'while the illegitimacy rates for the lower classes and minority races have slowed their rate of increase and the illegitimacy rate for adolescents has declined, the phenomenon has occurred with increasing frequency among the older, better educated and economically privileged groups'.[2] In Great Britain, too, there may appear to have been an increase in unmarried pregnancies in the middle and upper-class social groups, although precise figures are not available, but in any case the overall illegitimacy rate continues to rise.

From 1915 to 1940 the percentage of illegitimate births remained constant at about 4 per cent of all live births registered. In 1945 a peak of 9·3 per cent was reached, with 63,420 illegitimate babies born. Six years later the percentage was back to 4 per cent, but since 1960 there has been a steady increase, as the table on p. 4 shows:[3]

Why does it happen?

In a way the increasing illegitimacy rate is puzzling. Contraceptives are now freely available, and even the most advanced advocates of permissive morality still agree with the whole bench of Bishops that it is unethical to bring an illegitimate child into the world. Why, then, do more and more single girls have babies? Who are the unmarried mothers, and why? Are some of them the helpless victims of unscrupulous men, and the rest naughty girls with no morals who are simply out for a good time? Do they come from broken homes? Are they psychopaths? Are they 'oversexed'? Or just dim?

All these suggestions contain some truth, but the real answer is more complicated and extremely difficult to find. Not very much has been written and still less research done into the causes of unmarried motherhood. As has already been suggested, some insight has come from the scientific study of human personality, and especially from Sigmund Freud's theory of unconscious motivation. This provided a clue which was enthusiastically followed up in the United States, and the results may be found described in various American publications on psychiatry and social work. In particular, Professor Leontine Young, in her book *Out of Wedlock*, based on a study made in 1943, suggested that with very rare exceptions every unmarried mother is motivated by an unconscious wish for a baby, and that this wish is geared to her relations with her parents. Dr John Bowlby's well-known report to the World Health Organisation, *Maternal Care and Mental Health*, confirms these findings in that it provides evidence of the harmful effects of the absence of loving parental relationships in

---

YEAR	NO. OF ILLEGITIMATE BIRTHS	PERCENTAGE OF ALL LIVE BIRTHS REGISTERED %
1960	42,707	5·4
1961	48,490	5·98
1962	55,376	6·6
1963	59,104	6·92
1964	63,340	7·23
1965	66,249	7·67
1966	67,056	7·9

(These figures need careful interpreting, however. There is evidence that fewer girls are getting married simply because they are pregnant, and hence the number of illegitimate *births* will be higher even if the number of illegitimate *conceptions* remains the same. Moreover, the total number of births registered has fallen every year since 1964.)

babyhood and childhood. Dr Bowlby says: 'The girl who has a socially unacceptable illegitimate baby often comes from an unsatisfactory family background and has developed a neurotic character, the illegitimate baby being in the nature of a symptom of her psychological ill-health.'[4] Clark Vincent, however, in a study made in California, showed unmarried mothers to be not markedly different from similar girls who did not become pregnant, although he also discerned the harmful effect of unsatisfactory home life and poor moral standards. In Switzerland in 1941 Professor Hans Binder found overwhelming evidence among the unmarried mothers he interviewed of psychological trouble resulting from disturbed childhood and unhappy home life, and more promiscuity than other studies have revealed.[5] In this country, Dr Donald Gough, also approaching the problem from a psychiatric point of view, regards unmarried motherhood as evidence of disturbed personality, although he does not link it so exclusively with the parents.[6]

It has to be borne in mind that psychiatric research can only be carried out with certain selected samples of all the girls who conceive illegitimately. Professor Binder's study was probably the most comprehensive yet made, as far as access to material goes, but even he was obliged to leave out of account a large number of mothers who could not be traced, had left the town of Basle, where he carried out his research, or who refused to co-operate. Other research workers have approached the problem from a sociological point of view, and in particular Miss Barbara Thompson analysed the records of 582 women who gave birth to illegitimate children in Aberdeen between 1949 and 1952. Her conclusion was that 'illegitimacy, like delinquency, thrives when social values, cultural as well as material, are low. Insecure family life, poor and overcrowded homes, lack of constructive aims and outlets, lack of general planning ability and permissive attitudes to extra-marital relations may all contribute to the occurrence. Such factors rarely occur in isolation, and it would be difficult to assess their relative importance in causing or favouring a high illegitimacy rate'.[7] Cyril Greenland, in two extensive studies,[8] found no clear evidence as to the causes of illegitimacy, but suggested that a combination of social circumstances, such as living away from home and opportunity for intimacy with men, could be conducive. More recently it has been pointed out that pregnancy, or even a false pregnancy, can offer an escape route for some girls when life becomes too difficult for them.[9]

More advanced research projects are at present being carried out in the United States into the psychosocial causes of unmarried motherhood, but they are hampered by two major difficulties: the lack of accurate measurement instruments and the problem of finding a 'normal' control group. An abstruse hypothesis has been put forward by Kasanin and Handshin: 'These pregnancies represent hysterical dissociation states in which the girls act out their incest phantasies as an expression of the Oedipus situation.'[10] Such theories may seem to have little relevance for the busy caseworker, but both singly and more especially when compared with one another, they help to throw some light upon the causes of unmarried motherhood, and in doing this, research will ultimately be of great importance to casework; it may, for example, produce some guidance as to which girls are likely to make good mothers and which would be better to part with their babies.

What is clear from experience, and confirmed by all the investigations made, is that there are in fact as many causes of unmarried pregnancy as there are cases – or rather that there is a unique combination of a number of contributory causes, which vary greatly in strength and subtlety, in the case of every pregnant girl. It is not possible to put together a set of external conditioning factors that will tend to put some women at risk. It would be nonsense to deduce, for example, that because Alice is the third child of a window cleaner living in a condemned house, in the 'C' stream at a secondary modern school and with a tendency to overweight, she is therefore likely to have an illegitimate baby. The deep sources of unmarried motherhood lie partly in the personality of the mother herself, and partly in the upbringing and home life that have formed her and continue to influence her. Hence the girl's parents are of primary importance in the situation; very often their need for casework help is at least as great as their daughter's – if they will accept it. In their attitudes towards her, and each other, are found what may be described as the predisposing, or primary factors, and in most instances of illegitimacy there will be found some degree of stress in this connection. But, again, the situation is complex and there are many forces at work. Shocked and bewildered parents will sometimes say in all sincerity to a caseworker: 'Please tell us where we have gone wrong. We've done everything we know to bring her up well,' and indeed it may be difficult to find any shortcoming in their family life. One feels deeply for the distress of such fathers and mothers. Yet there are two sides to every relationship, and the girl herself may have reacted in some unpredictable way. For example, it has sometimes happened that the daughter of united and loving parents has formed the idea that she is not really wanted for herself, and if this grows into a strong teen-age fantasy she may act it out by looking for what she hopes will be real love elsewhere. Much simpler is another parental reaction: 'Why has she done this to us? We've always given her everything she wanted.' The child has clearly been spoilt, and is now accused of ingratitude. 'Only' children in otherwise good homes are often over-protected. The girl who goes to the cinema with her mother on Friday nights, and is met by Father as she comes home from the Youth Club, cannot learn to stand on her own feet, and is likely to seek her own way to freedom.

There is also a good deal of 'secondary neglect': parents are concerned for the material welfare of their daughter, yet they make no attempt to share her interests or help her to formulate ideas and standards of her own. Annette's mother, for instance, went out to work so that the family could have a car; Annette was given pretty dresses and a transistor and more pocket-money than most of her friends. At fifteen she had intercourse with her boy-friend because all her peers at least talked as though everyone did, and was furious at being 'caught'. Her parents had never shared their own thoughts with her, nor offered her any constructive teaching as to what life is all about and what sort of objectives are worth striving for.

A high proportion of pregnant girls have stepfathers or stepmothers, relations with whom vary from excellent to not being on speaking terms. Parental disharmony is fairly frequently found in the history of unmarried mothers – although, as with all the other factors, too little is known about its incidence in their homes compared with those of girls who do not become pregnant. In itself it seems to be less important than the attitude of the parents towards their daughter. Either can be jealous of her youthful attractiveness and her opportunities in life, and either can regard her as a rival for the affections of the other. Leontine Young in *Out of Wedlock*[11] puts forward her theory that 'the great majority of unmarried mothers come from homes dominated by the mother', and this hypothesis, unlikely as it may seem, does help to throw light on some otherwise inexplicable situations.

Doris, for example, was referred to a social worker when she was six months pregnant. She was eighteen, lived with her parents and two brothers, and worked in a garment factory. She described how she had met Joe at a dance, and had intercourse with him at the second and three subsequent encounters. She had not told him of the pregnancy for the simple reason that he had left the district; he worked for a firm of contractors and the job was finished. She did not know his surname or whether he was married, but had an idea he came from Scotland. Doris was not in the least perturbed, even though she 'thought she'd have to have it adopted'. Indeed she conveyed her feeling that the whole thing was somehow inevitable, and she was almost relieved that it had happened.

Closer contacts with Doris and her family revealed that her father was on shift work in a local pit; he was a quiet man who retired behind his paper when he was off duty and left the running of the home and family to his wife. Mrs Birch was a very capable woman; indeed Doris was undeniably 'mother-ridden', to use Professor Young's word. On learning of her daughter's pregnancy Mrs Birch immediately took control of the situation: 'She's not the first and she won't be the last,' she declared, and announced that the baby should be born in the local hospital and she herself would bring it up. Doris, to her surprise and indignation, disagreed. She would go to a Mother and Baby Home and offer her child for adoption. Open conflict arose in the family for the first time; Doris won to the extent of going away from home, but when her mother visited her after her son was born, she very quickly agreed to keep him – or rather to let her mother do so.

Leontine Young's interpretation of this kind of situation is that Doris's pregnancy was a more or less conscious rebellion against her domineering mother. She wished either to assert her own freedom and initiative in protest against her mother's relentless management of every detail of her life, or perhaps to make her mother a placatory offering of a baby. In any case the whole episode took place in relation to her mother; at no time did she see the child as a real person in his own right, and the 'man from Scotland' was merely a means to an end.

This does help to explain two puzzling features that many case histories display: first, the strangely detached attitude of the girl towards the actual begetting of the child (quite often she insists that she had a 'blackout' and remembers nothing of it); in psychiatric terms, this is a true denial or repression of an unacceptable fact, and not merely a façade against prying or criticism from other people.

Secondly, there is the slenderness and brevity of her contact with the putative father. Professor Young's theory is that nearly all unmarried mothers are motivated by a fantasy-wish for a baby, out of wedlock, without a man, and will go to great lengths to get it. This generalisation is certainly over-broad, since it leaves out of account the many unmarried mothers who are not mentally sick at all, but have, for example, anticipated an expected marriage. But it does perhaps provide a clue as to the reason why so few ever use contraceptives.

It is almost as though intercourse and conception were two different and unrelated things. In the eyes of the world, intercourse is acceptable, but conception isn't. Thanks to contraceptives, one can have the first with little risk of the second; but many potential unmarried mothers seem to be unconsciously looking for conception without intercourse. For them, contraceptives are irrelevant; they are the answer to the other question, the question of sexual connection, and they are not interested in that. The *avant-garde* in morals may make a deliberate decision to sleep together, and take suitable precautions to avoid the consequences, but when Brenda is getting ready for the dance on Friday night she would not dream of protecting herself against Ken's advances. To do so would be to admit that they are likely to have intercourse before she comes home again, and she cannot do this, because it touches upon her fantasy-wish for a child. There is, so to speak, a brick wall in her mind which prevents her from reasoning about her behaviour. 'There can be no doubt that the drive which propels an unmarried mother results in compulsive action,' says Leontine Young, and compares her to a sleep-walker. 'The serious problem,' she continues, 'is that her urge for a baby has been separated from its normal matrix, love for a mate.'[12]

It is obviously not true, though, that the unmarried mother's motivation is always unconscious. For example, there is a certain small proportion of women who quite deliberately set out to have a child without a husband and are prepared to face the consequences. There are others, more naïve, who give in to their boy-friends' advances because they hope it will lead to marriage if they do, and others again who trust their lovers' assurances that they 'won't do them any harm'. Marlene flounced out of the house after an argument with her father, and seduced her boy-friend as an act of defiance. Countless teen-agers experiment out of curiosity, happily convinced that nothing will happen to them. Moreover, it is possible for social workers and psychologists to become so preoccupied with the unconscious that they lose sight of the obvious, and quite forget the simple, strong biological urge to mate and the overwhelming desire to give physical expression to love that so easily dominate the behaviour of young people.

It is clear, then, that the sources of illegitimacy may be found in drives and motives of many different kinds, conscious and unconscious. A pregnancy may be accidental in the sense that although intercourse was intended conception was not. On the other hand there are girls who seem predisposed to unmarried motherhood, and in their histories it is often possible to trace causative factors of three kinds. In the first place it is likely that there are shortcomings in home and family life, and particularly in the daughter's relationships with her parents. It is perhaps especially the girl who gets on badly with her dad who is likely to give herself to her boy-friend in headlong uncalculating passion. Secondly, there may be qualities in her own personality that make her especially vulnerable: insecurity, for example, may give rise to a hunger for love or a need to prove herself equal with other people. But these factors by themselves do not necessarily produce an illegitimate pregnancy; it is equally possible that the girl's protest against adversity will take the form of petty larceny, drink or drug-taking, or be stored up until she has children of her own to work it out upon.

Before the pregnancy occurs, a third set of precipitating circumstances will come into play. Quite obviously, there must be a man available and willing, and opportunity for intercourse to take place. Casual encounters at dances and the pictures provide these easily enough for many girls. But a host of more subtle factors may also help to tip the balance: jealousy of a married sister's pregnancy, spite, defiance of social conventions, rejection by another boy-friend or even a row with the boss at work, for it is often a single minor incident or loaded word which triggers off the final reaction. Quite often she has had too many unaccustomed drinks.

At all events, there will be found a unique set of causative conditions leading to the pregnancy, and these will be of three kinds: first, the primary predisposing factors which are latent both in character and in family relationships, and then the precipitating circumstances in the form of specific impulses, emotions and events. Many psychiatrists and sociologists are trying to isolate and assess these factors scientifically, but they confront the caseworker embodied in human individuals.

They may be young or not-so-young, distressed or outwardly indifferent and are as varied in their situations as they are in appearance.

Jane, whose I.Q. was about seventy, was herself illegitimate; her mother later married, but after her early death Jane had been handed from grandmother to aunt and had spent a period of eighteen months in a children's home. At the age of thirty-six she is an amiable person, quick to form superficial relationships, and an excellent worker in a hospital kitchen because her mental make-up is such that she is always willing to do whatever she is asked to do. And for exactly the same reason she is now expecting her fourth illegitimate baby as a result of going for a walk with the cook.

May was a very different person, intense and unstable in temperament. She had grown up in poverty because her father was a chronic invalid, had outstripped her family by going to Grammar School and College of Further Education, and was quite unprepared for the wider world in which she found herself. As a newly qualified teacher she fell desperately in love with another member of the school staff, unconsciously seeking security in the arms of an intellectual, idealistic young man who was in fact no stronger than herself.

Brenda, by contrast, was consciously looking for love; she had been brought up by a stepmother and had never felt that she belonged, or was wanted, anywhere. She was shy and unattractive; finding her first boy-friend at the age of twenty, she gave in rather unwillingly because she 'hoped he'd marry her if she let him'.

As Virginia Wimperis says: 'If we try to study why illegitimate children are brought into the world we must do it very humbly. No one ever completely understands another; motives are complex; forces of social pressure, religious belief, emotional relationships within the family, private fears and longings, act in an entirely individual fashion on the individual girl, according to her hereditary make-up, her upbringing and the degree of her integration as a person.'[13]

What can be done?

Our current social conventions do not help to prevent illegitimacy. We are greatly preoccupied with sex – but principally in its cruder manifestations. The physical act of coitus and its corollaries, contraception and abortion, interest us intensely, but we pay less attention to the psychological implications of manhood and womanhood, vital and fascinating though these are, and to the subtleties of enduring married love. Now that birth control is a reality we have become less preoccupied with the negative aspect of the moral law; 'thou shalt not commit adultery' has been overtaken by concern about the disabilities of the illegitimate child. Hence we conclude that if two people decide to have intercourse that is their own affair. They probably will as it is such a desirable experience, and no blame attaches to them so long as no child results. This is where we make a blunder in ignoring psychology, since the sexual experience is for a woman more likely to be a long-term process, not completed until the child she conceives has been born, suckled and weaned. Moreover, she tends to give more to her man than her body merely, and so for her fulfilment she needs the security of a permanent relationship. We forget this too often.

This permissive atmosphere is no help to young adults who are preoccupied with exploring their own potentialities, especially those who are predisposed towards unmarried parenthood. Margaret Drabble has contended in an article in *The Guardian* that contraceptive techniques have at last brought freedom to women: 'Emancipation is now a reality and we ought to be entering on the golden age of free adult sexual equality and companionship that the feminists fought for.'[14] A week later there appeared the following letter:

Sir,

How will I know when the permissive society arrives at N.13?

Yours faithfully,

N.13 Unmarried Mother.

So we are not as free as all that. Women can now have sexual relations, if they wish to, with little fear of conceiving a child, but this fact does not in itself seem to be much of a start to a golden age. It is no more than a cruel irony to those who are not able to manage contraceptives, and no allowance is made for chance or human impulsiveness. As the writer of the letter quoted above has found, even the permissive society is not happy about the birth of illegitimate children – nor should it be. The issues are complicated and many of us still find it difficult to be objective. The pregnant girl has broken the traditional Christian precept of chastity. Many people are now indifferent to this consideration, but in others it still arouses a furious and unreasoning wrath, and in some a compassionate concern to help. She has brought embarrassment on her family and disgraced herself;

this makes most of us feel uncomfortable. And she has brought into the world a child she cannot support; this triggers off all the reactions centred upon our pockets and bank balances. We can only wish she hadn't, or condemn her out of hand.

Her partner comes in for much less public attention. Under the double standard of morality that obtained in Victorian days, the young man sowing his wild oats was indulgently regarded, but his sister was expected to remain pure – otherwise, woe betide her. Josephine Butler and Ellice Hopkins led the campaign to alter this way of thinking, but traces of it are still with us. Michael Schofield[15] confirms that most teen-age boys, although they themselves thought it right to have sexual experience before marriage, nevertheless want to marry a virgin. Many boys divide girls into two types: the sort that are 'good for a bit of fun' and the sort they propose to marry, whom they expect resolutely to wait for the wedding-ring.

The double standard has indeed changed in the opposite direction to that intended by the nineteenth-century reformers, who wanted men to be as chaste as they expected women to be. Among those who consider themselves emancipated from old taboos it is now acceptable for anyone of either sex to have intercourse, provided that the partners genuinely love and respect one another, and mutually consent. The pamphlet *Towards a Quaker View of Sex*, published in 1963, and the British Council of Churches' Report on *Sex and Morality* in 1966 are surely right in stressing the importance of the nature of the relationship rather than the marital status of the partners. The question has been asked with great sincerity: Which is worse – that an unmarried pair who cherish one another should give physical expression to their love, or that a married couple should continue to have intercourse when love between them has died? Coitus, the Quakers suggest, should be 'a consummation, a deeply meaningful total expression of a friendship in which each has accepted the other's reality and shared the other's interests. . . . This would mean that each cared deeply about what might happen to the other and would do everything possible to meet the other's needs and lessen any suffering that had to be faced.'[16]

Yet there is more to be said. The whole essence of being in love is that the lover is convinced that This is It, that he and she are destined for one another and nothing shall ever separate them. But six months later it may prove to have been all a mistake. How are they to cope with an experience so bewildering? There are a great many sorts of love, although the English language has only one word for them all. Too little is said about the deepest and most real, which has no self-regard in it at all and will make any sacrifice for the well-being of the other. In particular, it will accept the self-discipline of restraining the physical expression of love because it will on no account subject the beloved to the risk of harm. The following poem from *Punch* makes the point with delicacy and charm:[17]

MODEL LOVE SONG

For a young poet faced with the problem of
rebelling against a permissive society
by Peter Dickinson

Ah, Miss Simpkins, oh! my saint,
Love me with a passion faint!
    Love me – but do not admit
    You would ever think of it.
Love me with severe restraint.

Weekly I'll invent a new
Delicate, precise tabu,
    Like some ornate Indian screen
    Which I then will place between
My attentions, dear, and you.

Should some authoress or don
Egg our baser instincts on,
    You will raise a pretty blush,
    I will vent a manly 'Tush!'
Then we'll share, perhaps, a scone.

Be, but do not be, my own!
Let us find some wrinkled crone
    Born before our beastly sires
    Loosed the bonds of their desires,
Hire her as our chaperone.

Ah! Miss Simpkins, you and I,
Heedless when our elders cry
    'Come and wallow, come and caper,
    Morals are but scraps of paper,'
Will live a month on half a sigh.

Judging by the solemn way
They embark upon their play,
    By their wearisome debating,
    Pompous tantrums, tedious prating,
We'll have much more fun than they.

What is to be done? In a world in which young people are free to experiment if they wish to – and where indeed they get every encouragement from the Sunday papers, pornographic glossies and television – is there anything that adults can do to protect the children they care for?

We easily assume that teen-agers take their standards of behaviour from one another, and regard anyone over twenty as hopelessly old-fashioned. This makes older people diffident and unwilling to give a lead, and the adolescents lose no time in pointing this out. 'Anyway,' they retort, 'you're just as bad yourselves; look at your divorce rate, your broken marriages, your adultery. Who are you to teach us?' The more honest adult feels disposed to retire in shame.

But this is a wrong approach. Experience shows that most teen-agers are, in fact, ready enough to listen to those whom they respect; and the qualities that win their respect are honesty and integrity. It is also a fact that caseworkers concerned with illegitimacy hardly ever have a client who has been brought up in an atmosphere of frankness and mutual trust by two parents who love each other and their children. The security of really good family relationships in childhood is strong enough to hold the teen-ager, whatever his encounters may be at school and university and in the factory, although this is not to say that he will meet no difficulties and have no perilous adventures. It follows from this that the prevention of unmarried parenthood begins at the nursery stage, where the foundation of every quality of character is laid. The child needs to grow through graduated steps in freedom and its complementary responsibility; 'smother-love' is as harmful as outright neglect. Also he needs to be able to discuss with his parents every question that arises to perplex him, from 'where does the bath-water go?' to 'what happens when you die?' He does not expect, after a very early age, that they will know all the answers: what he does expect and need is a sympathetic hearing from a thoughtful adult who will take him seriously as a person. In this way he will 'catch' the attitude of his parents and teachers towards such questions as divorce and abortion. If they are fair-minded, receptive to new ideas, concerned about moral standards and concerned also about people, the two generations will have much to say to one another. But adults must clear their own thinking, set their own standards and let their lives be seen to conform to them, before they can hope to help the young to attain the maturity they need in order to live in true freedom.

'I'm going to have a baby'

What does it feel like to know that you are going to become an unmarried mother? Reactions depend largely upon the reasons underlying the pregnancy. Girls like Doris (p. 7), although for decency's sake they may assume at times a suitable air of shame, are at heart triumphant rather than dismayed. People cannot fail to notice them now; so they sit quite still at the centre of a storm of reproaches, inquisitions, arguments and altered arrangements, enjoying their moment of power. They will not plan realistically for their baby, for he is nothing more than a tool to be used in the grand defiance. If Mother wants to bring him up at home they insist – for a time – upon adoption, and vice versa. Such girls seldom grow much in wisdom or maturity through their pregnancy, and indeed are very likely to embark upon a second one sooner or later.

For far more girls, though, the first signs of pregnancy mean dismay and panic. Many look back to the first weeks as the worst part of the whole ordeal, when certainty grows as day follows day, but no one else in the world knows about it. The boy-friend is often the first to be told. He may say in the first shock: 'We'll have to get married,' and at a later stage struggle to extricate himself fom this rash promise. He may (perhaps not realising the extent of his cruelty) ask cynically what it has to do with him. Or he may advise his former girl-friend to 'get rid of it', even suggesting what she should buy from the chemist or whom she should consult.

Very few pregnant girls known to caseworkers have sought an

abortion. Perhaps the two are mutually exclusive as possible solutions, since the girl who decides to terminate her pregnancy must take action within the first eight weeks, and it is unusual for a client to approach a caseworker before the third month. Even so, the expectant unmarried mother who has tried and failed to abort is rare in the agency lists. This may be evidence of the strong unconscious wish for a baby already discussed. It would appear that by and large the abortionists' clients are those who conceive accidentally, whereas those who approach the social worker include not only those who reject abortion as a possible means of rectifying a mischance, but also most of those who are subconsciously motivated towards pregnancy.

At the time of writing it is too early to say how the Abortion Act of 1967 will affect the illegitimacy figures. There is evidence that more unmarried girls are having their pregnancies terminated than was the case before the Act was passed; many of these would have gone to a back-street practitioner if they had been unable to obtain an abortion legally. Moreover, a great deal depends on the views of individual gynaecologists. Some are interpreting the Act very liberally, some require a report from the Medical Social Worker, and others will still operate only for urgent medical reasons. Experience has already shown that in many instances where a case might have been made out for a therapeutic abortion, as for example when the patient was under sixteen years of age, the pregnancy was not diagnosed until it was too late. On the whole it seems unlikely that there will be any spectacular decline in the illegitimate birth-rate as a result of the Act. Many girls instinctively recoil from the idea of terminating the pregnancy even if it was not originally intended or desired, and although others may make half-hearted attempts to abort themselves, they stop short of asking the help of someone else in doing so. Few caseworkers, whatever their religious or moral principles, are wholeheartedly in favour of abortion on demand.

For many pregnant girls, the first weeks involve almost intolerable strain, leading sometimes to thoughts of suicide. Anxiety about whom to tell, and how, is mixed with black remorse and dread of public opinion, and intelligent planning is impossible in these early stages. This is a time when casework help is most urgently needed. Many girls say they have a feeling of unreality, a nightmare quality which sometimes persists until they are able to resume normal life again. As the months pass, some mothers-to-be slip into the state of contentment that accompanies a wanted pregnancy, but in many others anxiety mounts from one crisis to another. It is surely not surprising that psychiatric investigations made during pregnancy produce such depressing results,[18] and it is reassuring to find Rose Bernstein pointing out that 'a girl may become an unmarried mother because she has had pre-existing problems, or she may be having problems because she is an unmarried mother'. Under such circumstances it is natural enough that she should manifest 'guilt, panic, suspicion and denial' which may not be a noticeable part of her normal make-up at all.[19]

Her self-respect often suffers badly. 'I'll never get married now. No feller's going to want me now,' sobbed Brenda, voicing what many girls feel. This feeling that she is a worthless creature whom no one will want to marry and everyone will look down upon, besides being extremely painful, can have a corrosive effect, flattening hope and paralysing effort. What is the use of picking up the threads of life again if you're no good to anybody? Brenda needs skilled casework help, and the social worker must be able to distinguish between the blow to the hopes of marriage, which are so strong in teen-age girls, and the dread of 'what people will think', which is largely subjective and a form of self-punishment.

Fear of public opinion is still a burden to most unmarried mothers. They dread the censure and scorn of their neighbours, and often see slights where none is intended. 'Everyone I meet says "good morning" to my stomach.' Very few girls are able to realise that they are projecting their own guilt feelings on to their friends, and it takes a great deal of patient goodwill to convince them that everyone's hand is not against them. In practice, whatever their social background, almost every mother who keeps her baby is agreeably surprised by the warmth of her welcome when she first returns from hospital or Mother and Baby Home. Neighbours call with small presents and ask to see the child, and the nine days' wonder soon subsides. Yet even the kindness and goodwill, if there is the smallest degree of self-conscious condescension in it, is wounding to the unmarried mother, just as it is to the coloured immigrant, and for the same reason: it drives home to both the fact that they are at the receiving end of other people's compassion and therefore in a vulnerable position. Further difficulties, psychological, economic and practical, begin to come later; some of the men at work, or partners in the dance hall, make it plain that they expect her to be 'obliging', and there is also the gradually growing loneliness of the girl who does not count among the girls because she is a mother, and is not eligible for the Young Wives' Group because she is not married. She belongs nowhere. And in this isolation she has to bring up her illegitimate child, somehow helping him to face the fact of his fatherlessness yet making no demands upon him for strength or affection.

Things are hard enough for her if she is living at home with her parents, but ten times worse if she is trying to manage on her own in lodgings. Even if she is getting substantial help from her baby's father, and few mothers can in fact rely on this, she will have little money to spare for clothes and relaxation, and she is tied to the child. Trouble with the landlady or a few days' sickness can cause a major crisis. 'I made a mistake,' said the mother of a six-year-old. 'If I'd known what it would be like for us both I'd never have kept him. I shouldn't have done it.' It is a major tragedy when mother and child have to part when he is two or three years old, yet this happens far too often.

The girl who offers her baby for adoption also suffers. Society may say that she took the easy way out by shuffling off her responsibilities, while she herself undergoes all the pangs of real bereavement without any of the sympathy and understanding that would have been hers if her baby had died. She is left with the memory of a demanding, helpless infant and a constant unfulfilled desire to know how he is getting on. Whenever she makes a friendship with a man she has to decide when to 'tell him', and wait for his reaction to the knowledge. How she herself finally adjusts to the experience she has gone through depends on her personality and the circumstances of her pregnancy, and also to a perceptible degree on the help she has received. Jane (p. 11) is completely vulnerable, and although she protests every time that it will never happen again, it does. May's (p. 11) deep feelings of guilt have gone underground for a time, but there is a great risk that in middle age her tendency to depression and neurosis will become more evident. Brenda's (p. 11) story is one of the happier ones, in that after four more years of loneliness following the adoption of her baby, she married the right man. Her appearance was transformed, her self-confidence increased, and her natural gifts as a wife and mother found an outlet.

A certain proportion of girls, probably those who were the healthiest in the first place, come through the ordeal of unmarried motherhood more mature, wiser and more understanding. Many are embittered, bewildered, distrustful or resentful towards men, frightened or frigid. Others try to compensate for hostility in their families by becoming 'man mad' and perhaps promiscuous. Daphne, who became pregnant at her training college where sexual relations were the rule and chastity 'square', said: 'I'd like to carry a placard through the streets, saying "Don't!" '

2. The Individual and Her Situation

Caseworkers have good reason to know that the more they learn of a client's personality and social history, the more uniquely individual the client appears. Sweeping generalisations about 'all unmarried mothers' are just as misleading as they are in the case of 'all old people' or 'every child'. Yet some individuals are found to have certain characteristics in common with others, and caseworkers do in practice make use of certain categories, which help them to sort out their clients. Jane Rowe classifies unmarried mothers into 'four, rather clear-cut groups. This does not mean,' she explains, 'that all unmarried mothers fall into a set pattern; far from it. Trying to fit diagnostic labels on to people instead of treating them as individuals is nearly always dangerous and misleading. However, a discussion of broad groupings does emphasise the wide variety of unmarried mothers and the impossibility of making meaningful generalisations about them.'[1] Miss Rowe's groups are: 1. Women cohabiting in a fairly stable union with the father of their children; 2. Those who marry after the child is conceived; 3. Mothers who do not marry the baby's father, but are relatively free from emotional disturbances; 4. The unmarried mother with personality problems.

Almost all of the pregnant girls who come to a casework agency fall into the third and fourth of these categories, and they, again, can be divided into seven broad social groups which will help to individualise them:

1. Those who conceive before their sixteenth birthday
2. Those over thirty years old
3. Those who have two or more babies
    (a) Those who are not promiscuous
    (b) Those who are promiscuous
4. Middle-class unmarried mothers
5. Those living away from home
6. Those whose conceptions are extramarital

7. Those who do not come into any of these classes.

Again it must be emphasised that these are not water-tight compartments, but merely a means of breaking down the mass of referrals in order to distinguish individuals in their unique situations. In what follows, the use of case records will help to indicate the nature and extent of the specific problems encountered by the worker, as they appear to her. In subsequent chapters, reference will be made to the casework aspects of some of the situations described.

1. THOSE WHO CONCEIVE BEFORE THEIR SIXTEENTH BIRTHDAY

The pregnancy of a girl under sixteen years old arouses especial concern, not only in her parents but among school teachers and others. There seems to be no basic difference in the factors leading up to the illegitimate conception in the case of a girl who has not yet reached her sixteenth birthday, but where younger girls are concerned there are three additional complications in the situation: first, the fact that the girl is under the age of consent, and therefore the man responsible is liable to prosecution; secondly, she is likely to be still at school, and there may be difficulties about finishing her education as well as disquiet about the effects of the pregnancy upon her classmates; and thirdly, she is manifestly too immature to take on the responsibilities of motherhood. This would be the case even if she had a good husband to help her to care for a legitimate child with no stigma attached to it, but her real situation is far more difficult than that.

An analysis of twelve casepapers relating to girls who conceived before their sixteenth birthday shows that four were 'only' children, two of whom were grossly over-protected by both parents, four had difficulty in relations with their fathers and two had domineering mothers. Three girls had stepfathers, and one, herself illegitimate, had been brought up by her grandmother; five were assessed to be of average intelligence, five perhaps above average and two below. Nine attended secondary modern schools, two were at grammar schools and one at a comprehensive. After confinement only two of the twelve returned to school, one to a pre-nursing training and the other for the last term before her fifteenth birthday. All the others went straight to work. With regard to the putative fathers, all except two were under twenty; one was fourteen years old. Three of the girls seem to have had a genuine love relationship and later embarked upon successful marriage with the fathers of their babies, but a fourth marriage ended in divorce after four years. Three seem to have been infatuated with a lad older than themselves, two were exploited by men considerably older, and two sought a physical relationship as an end in itself. Intercourse occurred out of doors, in cars, in the girls' own homes, while out baby-sitting and on a ship in dock. What happened to the babies? Four were legally adopted, one by his mother's sister and one after fourteen months of fostering in the vain hope that the maternal grandfather would allow the child to go home. Two babies died; the remaining six went home with their mothers, and were to a greater or lesser extent taken over by their grandparents.

In casework with under-sixteens, the parents are likely to be at least as prominent in the picture as the child-mother herself, although family situations show the same wide variety as is found in other problems of illegitimacy. The four domineering fathers shown in the case records already referred to were rather similar in personality; they had shown pride and joy during their daughters' babyhood and early childhood, but as puberty approached had become more authoritarian and demanding, and the girls, troubled by this change of attitude, rebelled. The fathers insisted that they had tried to prevent this very disaster by stringent rules about what time their daughters had to be in at night, where they went, and with whom. Family rows followed, and defiance hardened. The fathers' possessiveness and jealousy towards their children probably arose from deep insecurity in themselves, and certainly had a great deal to do with precipitating the crisis.

Under the Sexual Offences Act, 1956, it is a misdemeanour to have carnal knowledge of a girl under sixteen years old, and a felony if she is under thirteen. Hence the caseworker may in the course of her work come to know that an offence has been committed. It has long been established that social workers cannot claim privilege in a court of law with regard to information received from clients, and hence she has a clear duty to report the facts to the police. How, therefore, does she stand with regard to her client's confidence? In practice, it is accepted both by the police and the courts that she will not necessarily pass on her information, and the professional relationship of social worker to client is nearly always respected. Good working relationships with colleagues are especially valuable under these circumstances, and where they exist, acute dilemmas seldom arise. The worker should have an understanding with the local superintendent of police; he is likely to point out that he is bound to investigate any information passed on to him, but will in practice allow her to use her own judgment as to whether she does in fact report to him. The worker thus has a great responsibility. Where it is a question of two fifteen-year-olds experimenting together, for example, it may not be in their best interests to set the processes of the law in motion; she must make her decision according to the circumstances of the particular case.

An important factor is the attitude of the girl's parents. They may feel so vindictive towards the man that her father will himself inform the police without hesitation; or they may prefer the worker to make the first approach for them, and this is often a good solution. In any case, when discussing this point, she has an opportunity to bring into the open their real feelings about the whole situation, and this may result in deeper therapeutic understanding between themselves and the worker. Mr and Mrs Black, however, were quite unable to face the possibility of police intervention. Susan had become pregnant while supposedly baby-sitting for a neighbour who was two or three rungs higher up on the social ladder, and they were partly in awe of him and partly concerned for his wife, whom they liked, as well as being unwilling to face the publicity involved. The caseworker therefore took no action. Shortly afterwards she was interviewed by the police, who had heard of the matter from village gossip, and invited to make a statement. She refused on the grounds that the parents were not offering any information and that she herself had not their permission to do so. The Deputy Chief Constable, judging from his notes on the file, evidently did not expect any other reply.

Where a charge is actually made against the putative father, the caseworker is in difficulty because of the convention that the same person does not visit both 'sides'. Here again good partnership with colleagues will be useful. If she can collaborate with a male Probation Officer to sort out the relationship between the two young people concerned, much useful work can be done, since the putative father is likely to be put on probation for two or three years. Has he lost interest in the girl already, or are they hoping to marry in due course? What is the real likelihood of this? These questions are very relevant to the future of the baby, as will be seen later. In the meantime the caseworker will counsel and support the mother and her parents through the court proceedings, which are even more dreaded in prospect than dreadful at the time.

The second complication is concerned with schooling. Pauline, for example, was a bright girl who hoped to be a domestic science teacher. At the time when she should have sat her 'O' levels she was nearly eight months pregnant. Her form mistress, although realistic and helpful in her approach, had a difficult time with the rest of the class, who knew the reason for her abrupt disappearance. Pauline went to a Mother and Baby Home where special coaching was available. For three weeks she was too restless to concentrate on lessons of any kind; then followed a period when she settled down and studied hard, saying that the school work was a link with what she called her 'real life', but this fell away shortly before her baby was born, and was not resumed afterwards.

The whole question of school work during pregnancy and after confinement is connected with the problem of the immaturity of the very young mother. Some attempt to continue with lessons is probably useful, not so much for academic reasons as to provide the much-needed security of the familiar that Pauline appreciated. In effect, early pregnancy usually leads to abrupt termination of schooling, because the young mother feels that her experience has separated her from the adolescent world and put her among the grown-ups, however little she may in fact have matured. She could not settle to lessons again. Even girls who had intended to train for a profession tend to abandon their plans and take the first job they can get, and it is often difficult to persuade them that they may later regret not having continued with their studies.

Young teen-agers are quite unprepared for the physical and emotional changes of impending motherhood, and when in addition to these the adult world reacts strongly to the new situation, the result can be deeply disturbing. As for the outcome, there is a great need for more factual knowledge than we have at present of the results of the various policies pursued. It would appear to be unrealistic for a girl who is returning to school to keep her baby; how can she effectually be a schoolgirl from 9 a.m. till 4 p.m., and a mother when she returns home? On the other hand how does a young woman of nineteen or twenty, about the time of her marriage, look back to the baby she offered for adoption when she was fifteen – and what does she think of it when she is fifty? At present we have too little knowledge to draw upon, outside our own experience.

The following two case histories may help to illustrate the points already made. The first is that of Pauline, who hoped to be a domestic science teacher. She was an emotional and spoilt girl, the only child of a skilled motor mechanic who ran his own garage, and the family lived in a modern bungalow. Her father adored his small daughter, and deliberately set out to give her all the things he himself had never had when he was a boy. Consequently Pauline had a great many toys and possessions which, as they were easily come by, she regarded rather lightly. Her father was at first hurt and disappointed, and later resentfully angry at her lack of appreciation of all that he did for her, whereas Pauline in her turn began to regard his presents as attempts to buy her love. Relations were very strained by the time Pauline was fourteen, and her mother was too ineffectual to help matters.

Then Pauline met Gilbert at the Youth Club. He was an apprentice fitter aged eighteen, who lived in a council house with his widowed mother and two younger sisters. Encouraged by her mother, Pauline took him home, but her father disapproved at sight of his clothes, his manners and his family and forbade the friendship, which thereupon went underground. Pauline's condition was discovered when she was four months pregnant, and after a miserable period of mounting tension while she was kept away from school and hardly went out of the house, she was admitted to a Mother and Baby Home sixty miles away. The family situation at this time was complicated, and tragic. Her father's need of his daughter's love, which arose from his own childhood insecurity, was completely unrecognised, and his love for her frustrated. He found himself unable to communicate with her in any way. Pauline's understanding of her father was almost nil; feeling guilty at having hurt him in a way she did not fully comprehend, and also fearing his anger, she put up a façade of defiance to hide her own bewilderment and isolation and her continuing attachment to Gilbert. Father and daughter erected glass walls round themselves, which Pauline's mother could not penetrate because she had too little insight into either of them. She took refuge in migraine from the monotony of nagging at them both.

Gilbert suffered also. He was forbidden to see Pauline, and her surreptitious notes tormented him because they reflected the confusion of her own feelings towards him. His mother, whose anxiety was tinged with jealousy, loaded him with reproaches. The caseworker's capacity for constructive listening and interpretation was much needed in the whole situation.

Pauline found that life in the Mother and Baby Home had its advantages. In spite of the petty rules and regulations, it was a relief to be away from the 'atmosphere' at home, and reassuring to find herself among other girls in the same situation. There was a feeling of friendly comradeship she had never experienced before, which helped her to cope with her own emotions. At first she accepted what everyone told her about it being best for the baby to have him adopted, but as time passed she determined not to part with him. When her parents visited she abruptly pushed John into her mother's arms, saying 'Here's your grandchild.' Her father seemed to recognise the son he had never had; two weeks later Pauline and John went home.

In the meantime there had been an ordeal at Quarter Sessions, in the course of which Gilbert had firmly stated that he hoped to marry Pauline one day. He was put on probation for two years. There followed another Court appearance, when an affiliation order was made against him for fifteen shillings a week. Some family adjustments were inevitable. Gilbert was allowed to come to tea on Sundays, but Pauline's father refused to listen to any talk of marriage. Pauline had got a job in the local Co-op, for she felt much too mature to go back to school, and teaching had lost its appeal now that she had a child of her own and hoped to be married. She shared John with her mother fairly amicably at first, but did less and less for him as her parents took control of the child. Grandfather, after a few weeks of resistance, set out to spoil him as he had spoilt his daughter, having apparently gained little wisdom from experience. When Pauline was seventeen and a half, she deliberately became pregnant again in order to force her father's hand, and she and Gilbert were married before the new baby was born. At last, with help from the parents on both sides, they set up house together, and four years later, when Pauline was twenty-two and Gilbert twenty-six, the marriage seemed quite successful. By this time they had a family of three children, but John stayed with his grandparents. He was a restless and demanding child.

Dorothy, by contrast, was herself born illegitimate. Her maternal grandfather was a casual labourer, and she lived her first five years in a condemned house until the family was removed under a slum clearance scheme. Her mother showed little interest in her, and when

Dorothy was two she married and went to live in Glasgow. Dorothy was left with her grandmother, an elderly woman of limited intelligence, and sick. She began to frequent the street corners when she was twelve, and on two occasions was taken home by the police. Granny always insisted that she was a good girl and gave no trouble. She was just fourteen when she became pregnant, and was referred to a casework agency by her doctor. It was clear to the caseworker that Dorothy should go to a Mother and Baby Home and that her child should be adopted, but neither Dorothy nor her grandmother could by any means be persuaded of this. 'It'll get fetched up all right, same as she was,' Granny insisted, and Dorothy echoed every word. The Children's Officer, whom the specialist worker consulted, was worried: Could the girl be regarded as in moral danger under Section II of the Children and Young Persons Act, 1933, or in need of care and protection under the Children Act, 1948? No adequate grounds for action could be found. Dorothy's baby was born in the local hospital and taken home at ten days old. The caseworker provided a layette and a pram, for financial resources were non-existent. Dorothy was not eligible for maternity benefit, and as she was under sixteen she could not even apply for Supplementary Benefit. Her grandparents' pension was the only income, apart from irregular sums sent by Dorothy's mother. When the baby was eight weeks old Dorothy got a job in a local factory, having just passed her fifteenth birthday and so escaped from the need to go back to school. This eased the financial situation somewhat, but left Grandmother in sole charge of the baby, a responsibility for which she was quite unfitted, and which provided a headache for the Health Visitor.

Casework with Dorothy was infinitely more difficult and less rewarding than with Pauline. Her intellect and background made it hard to establish any real contact with her, and moreover the caseworker was hampered from the start by having to help forward arrangements which she did not really approve of. Here is an illustration of the hard maxim that 'you can only start where your client is and go as far as you can persuade her to go'.

2. THOSE OVER THIRTY YEARS OLD

The older women referred to one particular casework agency fell into two sharply divided categories: either they were mentally subnormal and expecting their third or fourth illegitimate child, or of high intelligence and some standing in their social background. The first type will be discussed later. The pregnancy of an intelligent, educated, mature single woman seems especially irrational; surely she at least ought to have had more sense? This indeed is one of her worst torments after the event has occurred – the feeling that she has made a fool of herself. How, then, does it happen?

Childhood relationships with parents seem less important as a causative factor among the over-thirties, and they are less likely to be carried away by impulse, but it may be that deeper, unconscious forces become more powerful. As she passes to her thirtieth and thirty-fifth birthdays a woman knows well that her chances of marriage are lessening, and her unconscious urge towards motherhood, with or without a wedding-ring, may grow stronger. Also, and perhaps more likely, she may be consciously seeking security in the face of increasing loneliness, for most of her friends are married and preoccupied with their husbands and children. A physical relationship with a lover does in fact seem to provide that security for many women, giving them the power and poise they need to sustain the heavy responsibilities they may be called upon to carry. It may be that among the over-thirties there is a high proportion of accidental pregnancies resulting from failure in the use of contraceptives.

Certainly the responsibilities are an important feature of the situation. Pregnancy may interrupt the career of a woman who is well advanced in her profession, and in addition she may be looking after her parents as well, whether she lives with them or not. The need for secrecy often seems acute when the crisis comes. A mother who is in an advanced stage of cancer must not be troubled by the knowledge that her devoted daughter is pregnant; but how is the knowledge to be withheld? The practical questions are sometimes exceedingly difficult. And if, as usually happens, the older woman must leave home some time before the confinement, where can she go? The average Mother and Baby Home is filled with teen-agers; she does not share their passion for pop music, and it makes her ordeal worse if she is expected to join in their life. Few can afford hotel bills and fees as private patients. The best solution is one that is usually hard to find: a welcoming, accepting private household where the expectant mother can go as a paying guest, within easy reach of a hospital where she will be confined. A very few families seem to have a flair for this and will take a succession of such visitors. They can provide a service of very great therapeutic value, for their calm understanding and ordinary courtesy may be the very thing most needed to assure a woman in an emotional crisis that she is still worth something as a human being.

It may be expected that the man involved will show some concern, since the older woman has often had a fairly durable kind of relationship. But for him the penalties of publicity are probably even greater than they are for her. More often than not he is living an apparently blameless life with his wife and teen-age children; he would not think of breaking up his marriage, and even financial help may be difficult to provide without his wife's knowledge. The pregnancy is rather more likely to bring to an abrupt end a connection of some years' standing than to lead to the divorce court.

Hence there is great social pressure on the older woman to offer her baby for adoption. Her lover may see the child as a huge threat to his marriage and his whole position in life, so that he is desperately anxious for it to disappear. The mother's family, especially her brothers and sisters, sometimes take the same view, and she herself can be unwilling to expose them and her parents to public embarrassment. The child may be a bar to her resuming her profession, and there is also the expense and practical difficulty of providing a secure and happy home for him. Yet, in fact, the older woman nearly always finds it infinitely harder to part with a baby than does the average adolescent. She has a much clearer consciousness of what is at stake – that this is almost certainly the only child she will ever have; must she renounce the status and the joys of motherhood as well as marriage? The decision is often agonisingly difficult.

When she was thirty-three, Miss R. lived with her parents. Her father was disabled as a result of a car crash, and her mother had become almost blind. Her two married sisters lived fifty miles away. Miss R. had a degree in science, and had given up teaching five years before to take up a highly paid and exacting post in a pharmaceutical laboratory near her home. There was a great deal to do in the house in the evenings and at weekends, and her father, never a very even-tempered man, complained bitterly from his wheel-chair. She got on well with her mother, but her life would have been hard and monotonous without C.B. He was a colleague in the laboratory with whom she had been on friendly terms for three years, a gentle Welshman who lent her records of the Chopin nocturnes they both enjoyed. She had met his wife and two daughters. The change in the nature of their relationship began when he took her by car to see her father, who was temporarily in hospital some distance away from home, and they had been lovers for a year when Miss R. became pregnant.

Her first reaction was that her parents must not know. What would she do? Run in front of a car, maybe, or simply disappear overnight? She felt it would be better for them to be left without her, not knowing what had become of her, than to know the truth. And how long could she risk staying at home? She was less afraid of her father seeing that she was pregnant than that her mother would perceive it, for although she was blind, as Miss R. said, she seemed to see all sorts of things that other people missed. The day came when Miss R. slipped out of the house, leaving a letter on the kitchen table to say she had gone away for a few days, and went to stay with Mr and Mrs Jackson, who were used to people in her predicament. She delayed writing to tell her parents the truth, putting it off from day to day. In the meantime they had difficulty in managing without her; the doctor brought in a Home Help, and contacted the caseworker. She obtained Miss R.'s permission to visit her parents, but before she could do so, the mother had in fact guessed the truth, as Miss R. had expected. The ensuing shock and distress were very great, but there was a turning point when the worker took Miss R.'s mother to visit her and left them alone together.

The worker also offered C.B. an opportunity to come and talk with her. He accepted gratefully, although in dread lest his wife should hear of it, and arrived in a great state of tension and fear. In the course of an hour he talked not only of Miss R., but of his concern about one of his daughters who was making poor progress at school, and of his marriage. He loved his wife, but she was an intensely practical, commonsense sort of person who could not share his feeling for music and poetry, and it was through their shared interest in these that he had become friendly with Miss R. He would do all he could to help her, but he was intensely anxious that the baby should not come home.

The baby was in fact offered for adoption. Miss R. returned home on discharge from hospital, and was surprised by the warmth of the welcome she received from her father as well as her mother. Her son was placed with foster-parents pending adoption; parting from him, she said, was the hardest thing she had ever had to do. But two years later she burst into the caseworker's office with a spray of roses – her wedding bouquet. She had met again a man she went to school with who was now a widower, and they had decided to 'make a go of it'.

Miss M.'s home background was not very different. An only child, she had lived with her father since the death of her mother twelve years before, and she was forty-two. She was secretary to the managing director of a large engineering firm, and sometimes accompanied him on business journeys. Once she spent a whole month in Italy with him, and there had a sudden passionate affair with an Italian six years younger than herself. 'It was the warm sunshine and the lovely surroundings. I was free every evening. And it was so unexpected, that I should be courted so ardently – at my age!' she said. Soon after pregnancy began her father became ill with heart trouble. She obtained three months' leave of absence from her job, ostensibly to look after him, but she did not tell him of her condition. He died six weeks before her baby was due. But Miss M., unlike Miss R., found that she could not part with her baby daughter. After a period of anguished indecision, she made her plans; she sold the house her father had left her, took another secretarial post in a large town well provided with day nurseries, bought a wedding-ring, called herself 'Mrs' and set about making a new life for herself in a strange place. It was full of difficulties; she was homesick and lonely, baby Diana had bronchitis, the firm she worked for went bankrupt. But when Diana was eight years old she felt she had weathered the worst of the problems, and it had all been worthwhile. Diana partly understood her fatherlessness, and her relationship with her mother, all things considered, was remarkably good.

3. THOSE WHO HAVE TWO OR MORE BABIES

(a) *Those who are not promiscuous*

Among unmarried mothers who have more than one baby, it is possible to distinguish two types, although it is often difficult to decide which category an individual girl belongs to: first, those who have apparently been looking for the sex act as an end in itself, being comparatively indifferent to the identity of their partner. These girls, although promiscuous, are not necessarily prostitutes. The other type are those who are comparatively indifferent to the physical process of intercourse, but are driven to have a second or subsequent baby by forces they are not aware of, as Leontine Young describes. The latter all show some degree of personality disturbance, although of widely differing forms, and almost all have complicating factors in their home background.

A selection of fourteen casepapers shows that only two of these latter types of girls bore all their children to the same father. One had four by a married man living with his wife, with whom she maintained a relationship for several years; the other, during a short and tempestuous period of cohabitation with her lover, became pregnant again immediately after the birth of her first child. For this mischance she blamed her mother bitterly for having brought her up on old wives' tales instead of biological facts. Two other unmarried mothers in this group show remarkable similarity in their situations. Both were the comparatively calm, level-headed members of large families who lived from one crisis to the next and thrived on rows, tears and dramatic scenes, losing jobs or throwing them up with abandon and always going home, broke, to Mum. The two Joans (their names were the same) lectured, threatened, worked and shared their wages and their clothes with anyone who needed them, although in many ways they were just as unstable themselves. Both kept their first illegitimate child, who provided yet another ground for dissension in the home. Both suffered from the taunts of their brothers and sisters when they became pregnant again ('I thought you were supposed to be the good one'), endured grief over the adoption of their second babies, and went on to mature into useful members of society, working enthusiastically at voluntary enterprises such as old people's welfare, Girl Guides and Church Youth Clubs.

Three other girls had fathers who were completely unapproachable, and must on no account be allowed to know of their daughters' pregnancy lest he 'put her out of the house'. There was a strong element of the Victorian tyrant about these men. Their tea must be put before them when they came in from work; after they had eaten they moved to a chair by the fire and disappeared behind the newspaper, having spoken barely two words to anyone. If anything displeased them they barked, and wife and children hurried to obey. One good result of this regime was that the families drew strongly together in mutual support, but the burden upon the wives of having to keep the peace between husband and children, and to carry all the practical, personal and economic burdens because he was so bad-tempered, drove at least one of them to the verge of a nervous breakdown. The daughters' first protest was effectually smothered when, having offered their first babies for adoption, they returned to a life different in no detail from what it had been before; hence, no doubt, the second attempt.

Kathleen was probably the most healthy girl, emotionally, in this group with more than one child. Her soft, ample figure was ideal for cuddling babies, and her eyes were warm with maternal love. She anticipated marriage with her fiancé, and Peter was the result, but his father chose to emigrate rather than to own him. Five years later exactly the same thing happened again. 'I really did think I was going to be married this time,' she pleaded. But this baby would have to be adopted; she couldn't ask her mother to look after another. Could she have the baby taken away so that she did not see it at all? She would love it too much if she saw it. She loved her little daughter too much anyway when it came to the point. Peter was delighted with his baby sister, and Kathleen was blissfully happy to stay at home on Social Security to look after them both.

Margery was the youngest of twelve children. She was eleven when her mother died, and since then she had lived with one or other of her married sisters. Her father also died when she was fifteen. Margery had evidently learnt how to keep on the right side of people while getting her own way at the same time; she found work distasteful, and was incredibly ingenious at avoiding it. She became pregnant at the age of twenty, and at that time was living with one of her sisters, Mrs Coe, who was also in the family's black books because of certain alleged irregularities between herself and some male lodgers. The father of Margery's baby was a commercial traveller whom she met at the cinema where she worked as an usherette. Mrs Abb, who as the eldest sister was regarded as the head of the family, did her best to ensure that Margery had her baby adopted, but Margery decided otherwise and brought Neil back to Mrs Coe's house. There was trouble from the start. Mrs Coe complained if Margery had a job and left Neil with her, and when Margery was out of work she grumbled because she was always out and never did a hand's turn in the house. Mrs Abb was a respectable person and did not welcome either of her disreputable sisters. Margery became pregnant again, by the milkman this time, and her second baby was adopted. Soon afterwards Mrs Coe was admitted to hospital and died six months later. Margery took over the running of the house for her brother-in-law and Neil and although her domestic standards were not of the highest she settled down more happily once there was a role for her to play.

(b) *Those who are promiscuous*

It is a perilous business to single out some girls and label them promiscuous, and unrealistic anyway, since no one can ever fully understand the deep springs of another's conduct. Nevertheless it is an inescapable fact that a number of women have repeated pregnancies by different partners, and among these are many older women of poor intelligence.

The general picture, as revealed by eighteen casepapers, is depressing. Promiscuity is very clearly linked with poverty and squalor, low intelligence and the almost complete absence of any positive family life. Parents are divorced, in hospital, in prison or dead. If the girl has a home at all it is likely to be overcrowded; one third are living in council houses, but most of the others in old streets or condemned property. With one exception – an intelligent girl from a very ordinary home who had tuberculosis – all had such low I.Q.s that they had dragged through school as an incomprehensible boredom which had to be endured. At least two of the girls, when registering the baby, were unable to tell the registrar the date of the child's birth. Since there is rarely a breadwinning father in the family, and if there is one he earns a very low wage which is inadequate for the number of children he has to support, poverty is inevitable. Under these circumstances, sexual experience provides a relief and release which is readily available and seldom frowned upon. It is a clear symptom of the need for security. The fact that comparatively few girls in this category become pregnant before they are seventeen or eighteen years old does not necessarily imply that they have not had intercourse when they were younger, but may be merely an indication of reduced fertility owing to inadequate diet and poor health. When they became pregnant with their second or subsequent babies only five of the eighteen were working, and they were employed as domestics in schools or hotels. Jane (p. 11) is an example. Most of the others were looking after the children they already had, for extreme reluctance to part with a baby is typical of a girl in these circumstances. These eighteen young women had fifty-four children between them, of whom four had died and eight were adopted. Ten of the children are known to have been in the care of the local authority or a voluntary organisation at some time, which is perhaps fewer than might have been expected; but it seems to be typical that there is a grandmother in the background. She is usually a bedraggled and defeated-looking figure, but she has her name on a rent-book and therefore can shelter her daughter's children, whom she accepts with easy good-nature as being part of the scheme of things. Two girls were apparently the backward members of better-endowed families, and had brothers and sisters-in-law who willingly offered them a home, and such care as they could give. Three of the girls under consideration had been married and were divorced, and a fourth married the father of her third child. Another married a widower several years later. All the others remained single, as far as is known.

Janet's home was a condemned hovel, one of a row at the end of a muddy lane, deep in the country. Her father, who had worked on the roads, had disappeared when she was about four years old, leaving her mother to bring up five children on National Assistance. Her staple diet during her early years was bread and jam for breakfast and tea, and egg and chips for dinner. She and her brothers and sisters were always caked with mud from the lane outside the door, for the only amenities were a coal fire in a small, high grate, and a cold tap in a cracked sink. Her mother sank into indifference very quickly. As Janet grew up she began to hang about the door of the public house at the crossroads two miles away, and by the time she was twenty-two she had had four illegitimate children. She refused even to consider adoption for any of them, and was most unwilling to supply even such facts as she knew about their fathers. On two occasions she went away to a Mother and Baby Home during her pregnancy, and friendly help, good food and plentiful hot water appeared to work a transformation in her. But a fortnight after returning home she was in the same physical and mental condition as before, with the new baby tucked in a corner of the sofa and the nappies hanging above the chip pan on the unguarded fire.

Pat was the seventh of eight children, whose father, formerly a miner, had silicosis. Her first illegitimate child was adopted by a married sister who shortly afterwards emigrated to Canada. Pat herself married at the age of nineteen, and in the next four years had three legitimate children even though her husband was openly unfaithful to her. Finally he left her, and she divorced him. The children of the marriage were received into the care of the local authority because she had no home for them; her father had died, and when the family house was due for demolition her mother went to live with a cousin. Her sisters did what they could for Pat, but they both had large families themselves. Pat secured the tenancy of a small cottage, and in the next two and a half years had three illegitimate children, whom she kept with her. She received a great deal of social work help from both statutory and voluntary sources, but the clothing and household equipment she was given had a way of vanishing overnight. The gas meter was tampered with, debts mounted and a typical problem-family situation developed. Then Pat disappeared one day, leaving a sixteen-year-old neighbour baby-sitting. The children inevitably were received into care, and months later there was still no trace of Pat.

New contraceptive methods are now being used to help those clients who have a succession of illegitimate babies. There is a moral problem attached to this: if Pat were fitted with an intra-uterine coil, would it not amount to giving her a free hand to be as promiscuous as she likes, without fear of the consequences? Her caseworker felt it to be a greater good that there should be no more illegitimate babies to grow up in her squalid home. Pat herself, having heard from a friend that the fitting of the coil was uncomfortable, said she wanted to be sterilised, and this was in fact done. Many doctors are willing to prescribe the Pill for unmarried patients who have had three or four pregnancies, but single women who would find it difficult to cope with oral contraceptives are now being fitted with a coil or loop.

4. MIDDLE-CLASS UNMARRIED MOTHERS

'The stronger the taboos, the more urgent must be the emotional needs of those who break them.'[2] If this is true, it will imply that in the professional and managerial strata of society, which the Registrar General distinguishes as Classes I and II, the unmarried mothers are more likely to be seriously disturbed, since it is here that the taboo against illegitimacy is still strongest. As Jane Rowe points out, these girls 'stand to lose so much by having allowed the pregnancy to occur'.[2] The disruption of personal and family life is much greater than it is in the skilled, semi-skilled and unskilled classes. Are they, therefore, more unbalanced? Here again, generalisations do not work out because the predisposing factors are too subtle and complicated. Out of twenty-two unmarried mothers whose fathers' occupations are included in Social Classes I and II, three had severe and obvious personality defects, two others were of lower-than-average intelligence, two showed an oddly similar and abnormal psychological and social pattern, three had dominant mothers, one a rejecting father, and two were suffocated by too-close relationships within the family. The remaining nine were probably quite well adjusted before the events leading up to the pregnancy began, although most of them reacted very strongly to their predicament in a variety of ways. It has been suggested that the precipitating circumstances very often involve some situation in which stress is clearly present, such as leaving home for the first time, and this does occur among some of the girls under consideration. Eight of the twenty-two were living away from home when conception occurred, but three of these girls had already been away for well over a year. Four, however, had parents who were gravely ill, and of these three died shortly before or after the confinement. The main immediate cause of the pregnancy, as far as it can be distinguished, varied from a genuine love relationship which had got out of hand, through being swept off their feet by an older or more experienced man, to jealousy of an older sister who was apparently more successful, and to the wish to conform to the customs of the peer group. It also seems that in the more self-conscious middle-class home, the mere fact of growing up physically is of absorbing interest, and preoccupation with this process is likely to include a strong desire to experiment with the new-found adult capacities for intercourse and parenthood.

However it arose, the pregnancy invariably caused the greatest shock and dismay to the parents. They usually consulted the family doctor first, and were referred to the casework agency either directly from him or through the medical social worker at the ante-natal clinic. In five instances the specialist social worker was first approached by one or both parents, who explained the situation, as they saw it, in great detail, and incidentally shed much light on the interactions within the family. Their first request was nearly always for a swift removal of the pregnant girl from her home, however recently she had conceived, before anyone could know; the need for secrecy was great. This panic dread of 'anyone knowing' indicates the parents' inability to accept the disaster themselves and to try to find a positive way through it. It is usually modified as time passes, but more than one girl's parents found themselves trapped by the lies they told. Valerie, her parents said, was working as a mother's help in Essex; it was not too bad when her schoolmates asked for her address so that they might write to her, but critically difficult when relatives proposed to visit her when they were in London. At the other extreme was a family who resolved from the start that no lies should be told. The girl's mother faced and overcame her dread of going out shopping and to church, and the sympathy and consideration she in fact received helped to lessen her own distress.

The caseworker's approach to her better-educated and comparatively articulate clients is obviously very different from that demanded by a promiscuous girl of low intelligence. Both have equal need of skilled help, and both make demands upon the imaginative understanding of the worker. Janet (p. 36), when asked how she came to be pregnant, took refuge in 'I don't know', but Valerie responded to the same question with a detailed explanation beginning 'Well, you see', but which nevertheless had its own evasions and revisions of the truth. With Janet it was necessary to use the simplest language, not attempting to offer her interpretations she could not accept, but Valerie was able and willing to acquire some insight into her own behaviour.

It is usually best to acknowledge the need for secrecy which is so strong among middle-class families, but practical considerations often make it difficult for the girl to leave home at once, and hence a breathing-space is provided in which the first shock has time to abate and workable plans can be made, as well as lessening the impression the pregnant girl often receives that she is being sent away from home as a punishment. Few Mother and Baby Homes can take a girl more than six weeks before her expected date of confinement, and it is often difficult to make satisfactory plans for the intervening period. As in the instance of the older unmarried mother, the ideal solution is a 'foster-aunt' who will accept the pregnant girl as a member of her family until it is time for her to be admitted to the Mother and Baby Home, but there are not nearly enough such people.

Seventeen of the twenty-two middle-class unmarried mothers under consideration offered their babies for adoption, and this bears out a general finding that it is usually the more intelligent and the more stable girls who are able to face the prospect of parting with their babies.[3] Two of those who kept their children had a clear intention of marrying the father in due course. Of the remaining three, one was consciously defiant in underlining her association with the father, a schoolmaster who was a married man; another was a classical instance of domination by her own mother, who took over the baby from the start, and the third had a complicated reaction-pattern in which the illegitimacy of her own mother was a factor.

Valerie has already been referred to (p. 38). She was seventeen and had done well at the High School. Her father was a computer specialist with a large industrial firm, and she had a sister aged eleven. Superficially, the family relationships were fairly good, and they had a high standard of living. There was a television and a radiogram, but not a book to be seen. The décor of the house was in the currently accepted idiom of good taste, but life was lived very much on the surface. Valerie and her sister were sent to Sunday School, and indeed Valerie had been put in charge of a junior class, but her parents never attended a church service. Her mother said: 'My father was a good-living man, but he was in pain for years with angina. If there was a God, he wouldn't let people suffer like that.' Valerie's father was an extremely competent scientist and conscientious as a parent, but he understood little about people. Valerie had declined to go out on family picnics from the age of thirteen, and became very critical of her parents for being 'square'. She decided on agriculture as her career, and accordingly it was arranged that she should take a course at the County Farm School. Before this, however, it was necessary that she should work for a year on a farm, and three months before she became pregnant she had in fact gone to a farm in Yorkshire. There she rapidly became involved with a boy two years younger than herself, a large, slow-moving lad who had been in the 'C' stream at his secondary modern school. Valerie could never explain his attraction for her, but perhaps he expressed her revolt against all the superficial 'niceness' of her upbringing. Her pregnancy was apparent from the start because she had pronounced morning sickness. It was arranged that she should go to a 'foster-aunt' as a mother's help, and in her absence the case-worker saw a good deal of her parents. Their endeavour to face the situation realistically, on a deeper level than they were used to, was painful, but they did gain some understanding. In the meantime, however, Valerie had found another boy-friend, and she kept in touch with him throughout her stay at the Mother and Baby Home. Her parents, more disturbed than ever, insisted that the baby should be fostered pending adoption, and brought Valerie home two weeks after her confinement. She resented this bitterly, for she was by now very sick emotionally. A month later she disappeared in company with the second boy-friend, and was ignominiously retrieved from Scotland where they had tried to get married. Eventually she made a fresh start on her farming career, and within twelve months was pregnant again. This time she married the young man concerned, and gradually stabilised, although with many setbacks.

Alison's father was the manager of a large hotel. He telephoned the social worker one morning requesting an appointment, and in due course arrived with his wife. It seemed that Alison had told them the previous evening that she was pregnant; they already knew that her boy-friend had been killed in a motor-cycle accident five weeks previously. They were at a loss; what was to be done? Alison came to see the social worker next day. She was a level-headed and intelligent girl, quite able to assess her predicament objectively. She was grieving for her boy-friend, Keith, and very much aware that she was to bear his child. She wanted to tell his parents, because the baby was their grandchild and she felt they should have some say in what was planned for him, even though she herself was convinced that, whatever it cost her, he must be adopted for his own sake. She carried out her plan successfully; she and Keith's mother comforted one another. Knowing that this might well be the only child she would ever have, Alison entered into the experience of her pregnancy and confinement whole-heartedly, and mothered her baby daughter with devotion until she freely gave her to adopters at six weeks old. This was in spite of assurance from 'both her mothers' that they would help her if she chose to bring her up herself. Five years later she was still unmarried, but a happy and mature person.

It is evident that the death of her boy-friend radically changed Alison's role in the situation. Had he survived they would probably have married, but without him she felt herself called upon to take a more mature and responsible part, and she played it in such a way that she was able to share her own peace of mind with Keith's mother.

5. THOSE LIVING AWAY FROM HOME

In small towns, unlike big cities, there are comparatively few girls who have come away to work and then fallen pregnant, but there are others who have left their own homes in other parts of the country to stay with relatives or friends because they are expecting an illegitimate child. Both alike, however, appear to the caseworker to be insecure and rootless, and they present special problems.

Irene, for instance, left her home in the Midlands as soon as she knew she was pregnant. She had been going around with a man, and did not at once break off her association with him when she learnt that he was already married. The pregnancy brought the affair to an abrupt halt. Her mother was awaiting a divorce from her father in order to remarry, so she felt herself to be in the way at home in any case. The friends she came to stay with were overcrowded already, and she did not feel herself to be particularly welcome there. The caseworker found her a residential job in a hotel, where she filled in the waiting months quite happily. Later she moved to a Mother and Baby Home, and her son was offered for adoption. But what to do now? She was determined not to go home, and felt she belonged nowhere; could she not have another resident job? she asked. The caseworker knew a farmer's wife who wanted help, but she lived in a very isolated place, and Irene was a town girl. She surely would not settle five miles from a 'bus or a shop. Irene went to see, said she liked it, and moved in.

She took to the life at once. Poultry, pigs, kitchen garden and sheep interested her even more than the housework. A year later she married a farmer's son; soon they had a farm of their own, and a new life of happy activity began for Irene.

Fiona, by contrast, was a pallid little seventeen-year-old from Glasgow. Her mother was so angry when told that she was expecting a baby that she and her boy-friend promptly ran away. He stole a car, and they drove south together until the petrol ran out. In a small village they persuaded an easy-going woman to take Fiona in, and when Sandy was picked up by the police, the superintendent asked the social worker to look after her.

There was everything to do for Fiona. She was wearing all the clothes she had, and they were very dirty. She had no money and no insurance cards, and although the house she was living in was condemned and overcrowded, she would not be persuaded to go home. When she was scrubbed up and provided with clothes, the worker took her first to the doctor, then to the Labour Exchange, and then in search of a temporary job. With the worker's help, Fiona wrote a postcard to tell her mother where she was – and she sent another to Sandy at Borstal, for she was determined to wait till he came out and then they would be married. The caseworker also wrote to Fiona's mother. Tentative arrangements were made for her to go to a Mother and Baby Home when her temporary job came to an end, but when the time arrived Fiona herself decided to go home. When the worker saw her off on the Glasgow 'bus, having provided her with the name and address of a colleague in her area, Fiona was in a militant frame of mind, prepared to do battle with her mother for her baby and her boy-friend. Two months later a postcard arrived at the agency office to say that the child was born and everything was O.K. But she still had a year to wait for Sandy.

When a girl comes to stay with an aunt or married sister, she is usually confined in the local hospital, and the caseworker is often asked to find a foster-mother pending the placing of the baby for adoption, so that the girl can go back home as quickly as possible. This is an arrangement that many workers are unwilling to make, because there is a risk of the mother disappearing and the child being abandoned. If she fails to keep in touch, the foster-parents may be put to considerable expense and anxiety, as the weeks pass while efforts are made to find the mother. The caseworker must use her own judgment in such circumstances; it is certainly as well to have the adoption arrangements well in hand, and a date in view for the placing of the baby, before the mother leaves the district.

Girls of other nationalities who have come to work in the area present a wide variety of problems, but there were relatively few of them in the district under consideration, in comparison with those met with, for instance, in Birmingham or London.

Joyce was a South African whose father had sent her to England for a year on leaving school, to stay with second cousins and see as much as she could. Her cousins took her to a succession of all-night parties at which drinks flowed freely, and Joyce conceived at one or other of them before she had been in the country for a fortnight. She left her relatives and took a job as mother's help in a doctor's family, where she stayed until she was admitted to hospital in labour. Her baby was fostered pending adoption. Joyce grew up and matured rapidly, acquiring poise and self-confidence, as it seemed, in a matter of weeks. She had time for a tour of France and Germany before she sailed home again, but the worker never heard whether she told her family how her education had been completed.

The difficulties of all girls who work away from home are accentuated in the case of those who are coloured. It is true that for the most part they are concentrated in areas where there are others of their own nationality, but the few who work in predominantly white communities are especially vulnerable by reason of their loneliness and isolation. Anda, for instance, had left her home in the West Indies sixteen months before. She was independent by nature, and did not mind doing her State Enrolled Assistant Nurse's training in a hospital where there were a mere half-dozen coloured staff members. But there was nothing whatever to do in her off-duty time; the nurses' home and the social club were all right in their way, but very naturally she wanted to get out of the hospital atmosphere whenever she was free, and the town's only amenities were a dance hall, two cinemas and bingo. The other nurses were friendly, and one or two took her home with them, but it was probably boredom and a longing for the lively spontaneity of home that constrained her to spend a night with a travelling showman whom she had hardly seen before. The resulting pregnancy brought with it many problems: where could she spend her waiting time, and what future could there be for her half-coloured baby? She had no savings, and it was impossible for her to go home, expectant as she was. She discussed her difficulties with a certain aloofness, as though the whole matter concerned someone else and not herself at all. In the event she was fortunate, for after spending three months as a paying guest in a family, and moving to a Mother and Baby Home where she did extremely well, her baby was placed with adopters who already had one West Indian child. But what of Anda herself? She continued her nursing career elsewhere, but her social worker was left with the feeling that the whole experience had been sterile and bitter. Anda gained nothing by it. When she signed her consent to the adoption she was still remote, regarding her own experience with detachment and indifference. Nothing at all was changed, in her or for her.

6. THOSE WHOSE CONCEPTIONS ARE EXTRAMARITAL

The number of women who are, or have been, married but who bear a child to someone other than their husbands is unknown, but the records of one casework agency show that approximately one illegitimate child in ten has a mother who is married or divorced. How does this happen?

Out of a sample of nineteen, two young wives became pregnant while their husbands were away in the Forces or in the Merchant Navy. Both had their own homes, and children of the marriage. It would be an oversimplification to ascribe their conduct to the loneliness of enforced separation from their husbands, although this undoubtedly was a factor. One wife had a particularly close relationship with her in-laws, but both her own parents had died during her childhood and she was greatly in need of an active, ongoing partnership in love. On learning of her pregnancy, her husband at once left the Merchant Navy, obtained a shore job and effectively took control of the situation. The child was adopted, and a new phase began in the marriage relationship.

Ten others of the nineteen were living apart from their husbands, although no legal separation order was in force. Eight of the ten had left their husbands and gone back to their parents' home, and this fact in itself indicates at least some degree of immaturity. Their complaints against their husbands included infidelity, cruelty, drunkenness and extravagance, but they themselves seemed to have in common a certain weakness and colourlessness of character, and their inability to take a firm line was very evident when they were trying to make plans for the baby and for their own future lives.

Eight of the ten ultimately offered their babies for adoption, but there is a peculiar difficulty in this connection which they found it hard to face. The law assumes that every child of a married woman is her husband's child, and hence his consent is required to the adoption of the infant. But this involves the wife in telling the husband whom she has left that she has had a baby by someone else, and apart from the emotional difficulties of this, it gives him grounds for divorce. ('And if he divorces me I won't get an old age pension,' said a woman in her early forties.)

The practice of the courts varies considerably, but in general their requirements have become more stringent in recent years. Under certain circumstances, for example when the husband is serving a long prison sentence or when his whereabouts have been unknown for a considerable time, it is still possible for his consent to be dispensed with if the wife can swear non-access – that is to say, that it was impossible for her husband to have had intercourse with her. Strenuous efforts are usually made to find the husband, however, and whenever it can be done he is interviewed by the guardian *ad litem* or his representative. It is not unusual for the husband to make a show of withholding his consent in order to make difficulties for his wife. This can delay the placing of the baby, as most adoption societies will require some indication that his consent will be forthcoming when the adoption is legalised, before they will take any action.

Margaret was a quiet, gentle person who had grown up with her widowed mother and five older brothers who were extremely protective towards her. She married a brusque, assertive man, and found life with him so intolerable that she returned home after eighteen months. There was no child of the marriage. She went out to work, and her husband made no attempt to see her again. Two years later she became pregnant by a married man. Her first reaction was a severe depression, in which she was incapable of making constructive plans. After the first three months she recovered to some extent, but remained quite incapable of facing the prospect of telling her husband about the child. Yet she could not possibly keep the baby, for her mother was seriously ill; as a solution to the dilemma she agreed to let the caseworker interview her husband. Charles reacted to the news of his wife's pregnancy with violently abusive language; why should he sign a paper to make things easier for his wife when she had been unfaithful to him? It would serve her right if she had to put it in a Home. Ultimately he agreed to give his consent to the adoption on condition that Margaret wrote to him herself, stating explicitly that the child was not his. He used the letter as evidence to obtain a divorce on the grounds of her adultery, and remarried shortly afterwards.

Seven women were already divorced when they became pregnant. They were in the same legal position as a single girl as far as the adoption of their babies was concerned, but five of the seven in fact kept their children. Two of the five obtained affiliation orders, and another two made private agreements with the fathers for the maintenance of the children, but none married the father. One married another man several years later. All of the seven had children of their marriage, but only two of the divorced women, and two of those who were separated from their husbands, had their own homes.

It is interesting that three of these four women who had their own households offered their babies for adoption, as also did a widow in a similar situation. Of these five women, three of the four who decided on adoption recalled their babies within a week of their being placed in adoptive homes. Martha and Olive were both subjected to a good deal of pressure by their respective families to give up their babies, and great precautions had been taken to prevent the older children from knowing of the new baby's arrival. 'It isn't fair to them,' their aunts and uncles insisted, and Martha meekly agreed. Olive was more unwilling, but still said that the infant must go. At the adoption society's office her ordeal was extreme: 'It's like being hanged!' she sobbed. When she got home she found, as Martha had also, that there had been a reaction in the family and everyone was saying what a shame it was for the poor little thing to go. There was nothing for it but to return the babies. In both instances the family stabilised and the children grew up happily. Hence it seems clear that adoption is not usually a practicable solution where the mother already has other children and a home of her own.

7. THOSE WHO DO NOT COME INTO ANY OF THESE CATEGORIES

Far from being the exceptional ones, those unmarried mothers who do not come under any of the headings already discussed are the most numerous, for they constitute the most 'ordinary' girls. That is to say, their ages are between sixteen and twenty-nine, they have never been married, are living at home, are having their first babies and belong to social classes III, IV and V; they, or their fathers, are skilled, semi-skilled or unskilled manual labourers.

Even here there is to be found a complete cross-section of personality types and family backgrounds, from the fairly normal, well-adjusted girl to the emotionally sick, from the intelligent to the dull, with parents who range from the loving and affectionate to the completely rejecting, and including on the way the rigid ones who 'only want the girl's real good', the jealously possessive and the insatiably demanding. And here again, over and above all the categories and characteristics, individuals spring to the mind's eye: Louise, who was so good to her invalid mother and yet longed for freedom to find a man and start a family of her own; squarely built, sandy-haired Diana, who fought gamely to control her gaggle of little brothers and sisters; Ellie, whose baby died; Mavis who was so callously jilted; Belle and Amy, the giggling, inseparable sixteen-year-olds who asked for all they got and learnt nothing.

What have all these people in common, besides an illegitimate baby? Nothing, seemingly. And yet at some level in their personality, conscious or deeply unconscious, there is in practically all of them a desire for love and security of a kind they have not known. Only in a relationship of complete and unconditional acceptance can they work out their fears and insecurities, and it is the caseworker's task and privilege to offer them, if they will accept it, a relationship of this kind.

3. The Unmarried Father

'Is she really mine?' Tim looked up with wide eyes from the face of his child. He was sixteen, Cynthia seventeen; the fact that they had a baby was overwhelming to them both. Obviously they were too young to marry – they had not thought of marriage except as a vague possibility in the future – yet they were parents; this person whose minute fists were clenched as she cried aloud was their daughter. 'It's shattering!' said Tim.

Comparatively few young men are thus able to experience fatherhood while the girl-friends whom they have made pregnant experience motherhood. There are obvious reasons why this is so.

Society's attitude

In the first place public opinion, though muddled, is essentially punitive. Certain levels of Victorian society expected young men to 'sow their wild oats', and today sexual experience is widely accepted as being normal among young people. But if a baby results, the adult world at once is full of threats. A century ago no condemnation was too strong for the 'heartless seducer', and even today many couples will explain that they 'had to get married'. It is almost universally expected that the unmarried father shall pay for his irresponsible behaviour. The two assumptions behind this attitude are, first, that he is in fact always heedless and selfish, and secondly, that he will do his best to escape the consequences unless he is firmly pinned down. There is resentment if he appears to get off scot-free. He can expect nothing less than the anger of her parents and the reproaches of his own. They may put pressure on him to marry the girl when he is unwilling to do so, or they may forbid him to marry her when he does wish to. Moreover legal action may be taken for maintenance of the child, and perhaps criminal proceedings may follow if the girl was under sixteen years old at the time of conception.

In the face of this impending punishment, it is not surprising if the unmarried father's instinctive reaction on first hearing of the pregnancy is to take flight. It is easy enough for him to do this by taking a job in another part of the country. Or instead of physical escape, when his girl-friend tells him of her misgivings he may respond with: 'How do I know it's mine? You can't prove it. You went with me; you probably went with other chaps as well.' This can be cruel, certainly; but it is seldom realised that the news of the girl's pregnancy is sometimes almost as severe a shock to him as to her, and like her, he is liable to panic.

As time goes on, his difficulties increase. He is often forbidden to see his former sweetheart, either because the door of her home is closed against him by her parents, or because she herself, being frightened by her family's reactions, says she wants nothing more to do with him. The girl becomes the centre of an agitated crowd of parents, relatives, doctors and social workers, but he is left outside in unrelieved bewilderment and guilt. Naturally he is on the defensive when, ultimately, they notice his presence sufficiently to demand money from him. The caseworker concerned is almost invariably a woman, and, therefore, he assumes, on the girl's side against him; it sometimes takes a good deal of tact and patience to break down his prejudice.

There is a great need for more men as caseworkers with putative fathers, for without the sexual barrier between them it seems much easier to establish a relationship, and the young man's need of help is very great. Captain Fred Smith of the Church Army asks: 'Why bother about the unmarried father? Are we going to see him merely as a source of financial help or because his attitude to the girl will help us better to deal with her, or is he in fact a person in his own right who has views and feelings of his own?'[1]

Who is the putative father?

'If every unmarried father is considered guilty until proved innocent, the man who might under different circumstances wish to participate and help is lumped indiscriminately with the man who wants only to escape the whole business. . . . Obviously there is no possibility of knowing what the unmarried father is like as a person, no chance of his real participation in the situation, until this accusing and punitive attitude towards him is abandoned.'[2]

The illegitimate child's father is often, indeed, a shadowy figure. His responsibilities were until quite recently limited to contributing to his child's maintenance, without any corresponding right to see him or have any say as to how he was to be brought up. Hence it is not surprising that he regarded the affiliation payment as a retribution, and avoided it whenever he could. The passing of the Legitimacy Act, 1959, however, gave him the right to claim custody of the child and also to have access to him, and the Adoption Act, 1958, gave him the right to make representations when an Adoption Order is to be made. This slight improvement in his legal position reflects society's growing recognition of his status as a father. This recognition is probably due in part to a more realistic attitude towards deviants in general, but social workers can fairly take some of the credit for it. The rights the father receives make it easier for him to acknowledge his responsibilities, even though in practice these rights are still unfamiliar. At the present time their exercise can not only cause friction between the parents and their families, as in the instance of Rodney and Sheila quoted below, but has also provoked major legal battles, such as the 'blood tie' adoption case. It would seem that although society is beginning to recognise that putative fathers also are human, the fact is going to take a bit of getting used to. Public opinion still seems more sympathetic towards the unmarried mother,[3] and indeed this is inevitable and right, since she bears the baby.

Very little research has been done into the identity and attitudes of unmarried fathers.[4] John Bowlby, working on an assumption that they are very often promiscuous, relates to them the conclusions of a research project into venereal disease, that they are 'often emotionally, sexually and socially immature', and points out that 60 per cent of a sample of promiscuous men had come from broken homes.[5] Virginia Wimperis, however, corrects the balance by pointing out that there is no evidence that comments about promiscuous men apply to putative fathers in general.[6] Leontine Young, stressing the fact that so many men either disappear without trace or refuse to answer letters asking them for help, considers that the unmarried father is 'in almost every case a counterpart of the neurotic personality of the unmarried mother. Their problems complement each other with precision, and unconsciously each has sought in the other an answer to his own neurotic needs.' As she points out, the sexual act may express other things besides affection, especially hostility.[7]

Margaret Yelloly, however, in her survey found no evidence of these very neurotic relationships. Eighty per cent of the unmarried mothers in her sample had known the putative father well, and only 18 per cent had a casual relationship or did not know the man at all.[8] It is natural that there should be some emotional and temperamental correspondence between unmarried partners, and hence it seems likely that the girl who wants a baby without a man will attract a man who wants to make a woman pregnant without being responsible for a child. The encounter between them will be of the slightest, although it does not follow that either is promiscuous. Again, the emotionally starved girl who is looking for love, and who makes herself sexually inviting, is likely to attract a philanderer who will lead her on to have intercourse with promises of marriage. Then she herself may weave fantasies about the relationship which are quite unrealistic, and cling with pathetic tenacity to hopes of marriage which have no foundation at all.

The fact that he has begotten a child is often of great importance to the unmarried father, and, as with his girl-friend, how he reacts to it will be connected with his original drive towards having intercourse. If he merely wanted his own gratification from the encounter he will run away from the consequences; this is true promiscuity. Jack's name was given to the same worker by three different girls as the father of their babies. If he had an unconscious desire for a child, this may influence his attitude towards adoption; if he had real feeling for the girl he may be intensely concerned for her welfare, but almost oblivious of the baby. The coming of the child may resolve doubts about his own virility; if he is very young, like Tim at the beginning of this chapter, he may be filled with awe at what he has done.

Tim was given the opportunity to participate from the start, sharing with Cynthia the early anxiety and helping her to decide the baby's future. The distress he suffered arose from the situation itself and not from the censure of other people who wanted to exclude him from it, and so he was enabled to learn and to grow instead of being embittered by frustration and guilt. Tim was an intelligent but slightly neurotic boy who had grown up with his mother and grandmother after his parents' divorce when he was four. He had been sent to boarding school so that he should have some male influence, but this had increased his feeling of rejection. He started work in a solicitor's office, and began to 'hang around like a lost lamb', as Cynthia put it. She recognised later on that her feeling for him was largely maternal, and during her pregnancy she once confessed that she found it hard work to have to cheer him out of depression as well as her mother and herself. She managed to convey to him that something more than dog-like devotion was needed, and as he realised that his strength could help the situation he gained steadily in self-confidence.

According to the Midboro study quoted by Virginia Wimperis, at least 40 per cent of putative fathers are already married, although in about 20 per cent of cases the marriages were regarded as having broken down.[9] This seems a very high proportion of married men, but it is certain that every caseworker meets them frequently. Some form of sexual difficulty between husband and wife is almost always present, and an infinite variety of complicated situations is possible. Desperate expedients are sometimes used to prevent the wife from learning what has happened, but when these fail, as they quite often do, a crisis presents itself in which the caseworker has a great responsibility. George's wife Eleanor, who was herself pregnant, talked of suicide when she heard that a girl who worked at the same factory was expecting a child by her husband. George himself asked the worker who was helping the girl to see Eleanor, and in the course of intensive casework both were helped to see the shortcomings in their relationship and to make a fresh start.

The putative father, then, may have the same sort of psychological compulsions as the unmarried mother, and his social background varies just as widely. He may be a carefree young man who gets drunk at a party, or he may be skilled at seduction. He may be devoted to his wife and family, but separated from them by his work or by service in the armed forces. It can happen that he and his girl-friend loved one another 'not wisely, but too well'; quite often they are motivated by teen-age curiosity. He may be looking for security or thrills from the relationship, and his behaviour is as likely to be tender as aggressive. He may be merely wanting physical intercourse, but it happens at least as often that he is anxious to prove his virility. In any case he is a man with full human rights to respect, care and consideration.

Casework help

The pregnant girl may at first be very unwilling to let the worker get in touch with the putative father, perhaps because she is trying to deny the fact of her pregnancy and therefore wants to shut her partner out of her conscious mind; perhaps the memories of her association with him are too painful; or she is filled with anger or spite and therefore wishes to withhold from him the experience of parenthood that will presently be hers; perhaps she is trying to shield him because he is married. Women social workers in one area were found to learn the identity of the father in anything between 30 per cent and 80 per cent of their cases, and by no means all of them are contacted. But there is a growing awareness that it is a blunder to leave the father out of the picture.

In the first place this is because his need of casework help is now more clearly recognised. He is coming to be seen as a person in his own right, with strong views and sensitive feelings as well as his peculiar problems. It has been said that many men have a sense of inferiority because they cannot produce babies. If this is so, it is likely to be exacerbated when they find themselves excluded from the experience of their own fatherhood.

Alec came to the worker in great anxiety. Did she know his girl-friend Elaine? The worker did not. It seemed that Elaine's pregnancy had been discovered three weeks before, and since then her parents had shut her up in the house. When Alec called, her father had threatened him with violence. She had managed to smuggle one letter to him, which he produced. It was a pathetic document which showed clearly the conflict between her love of him and her fear of her parents; it ended 'I never want to see you again, but I will never ever forget you.' Alec had had ideas of abduction and elopement; he could not understand her parents at all, and still less Elaine herself. The vicar of the parish knew the family, but he could make no impression on them. They had closed their ranks to such an extent that the baby was born in the house, and they would accept no help of any kind. Nothing practical could be done for Alec, but at least he found in the worker and the vicar two people with whom he could share his distress, which was great.

Rodney was more fortunate in the long run. He resolutely refused to be pushed out during Sheila's pregnancy, and when she talked of adoption he made it plain that he would apply for custody of the child if she did place him. In the event, Sheila kept the baby, but it was only at the insistence of the Ministry of Social Security that she applied for an affiliation order. When it was made, Rodney applied for, and obtained, access to the child for two hours every Sunday. There was such dismay in Sheila's family that they thought of leaving the town altogether. Appeal against the decision proved to be so difficult and costly as to be out of the question; Queen's Counsel gave it as his opinion that a Chancery Judge would take the view that an illegitimate child should know who his father is, and therefore would be unwilling to rescind the Order. Ultimately a working arrangement was made with the help of the caseworker, and Rodney called every Sunday afternoon for his son. 'It'll just last till he gets another girl-friend,' said Sheila's mother, but there was in the event no other girl-friend, and four years later Rodney and Sheila were married.

A second strong reason for the present increase of interest in the putative father is that it is a great help to good adoption arrangements if his co-operation can be secured, for facts given about him by the mother are often very vague and sometimes prove to be quite inaccurate. Moreover, medical information about the father and his family may be very important, but cannot be obtained unless he agrees. If it is simply assumed that he will be unco-operative some vital facts may be overlooked, but a reasonable approach is very likely to be reasonably met. Again, some knowledge about his father may be valuable to the adopted child as he is growing up, and this can be given to the adoptive parents. The father, for his part, if he shows concern for the upbringing of his child, is entitled to as much information about the adopters as is given to the mother.

Finally, even to rate the putative father at the lowest level as merely a source of money, he is much more likely to be helpful if he is treated as a person, with his own views on the situation and his own problems.

But how best to approach him? This is sometimes difficult for a woman caseworker. There is a great risk of letters sent to a home address falling into the wrong hands, and by no means all men can be reached on the telephone. Sometimes the pregnant girl can be invited to bring her boy-friend with her, or he can be contacted at work. But whatever means are used it is essential that the first approach should give the impression that the worker is concerned to be helpful and not merely demanding:

Dear ——,

I have recently been asked to help someone who is known to you with a personal problem, and I am writing because your name has been mentioned in our conversation.

I wonder whether you, yourself, might care to discuss the situation, informally and in confidence? I shall be very pleased to help in any way I can.

If you would like to come and see me, I shall be in my office on . . . day at . . . p.m., but if you would prefer some other time or place, please let me know.

Yours sincerely,

When the young man does arrive, he must first of all be put at ease by the worker's reception of him. Then it is essential to define the situation clearly at an early stage in the proceedings. The putative father should be told that, although the worker will not willingly give evidence against him, it is always possible that she may be subpoenaed by a solicitor acting on behalf of the girl. Hence the father should not make to her any admission that the child is his unless he is prepared for this to happen. The threat of legal involvement can be a subtle but most persistent obstacle to the forming of a casework relationship, and may go a long way to explain the reluctance of some social workers to undertake work with unmarried fathers.

Probably the father's first need is for information as to where he stands. His rights and responsibilities should be explained to him, and in this the caseworker's approach is most important. It should be clear from her manner that she is concerned to see how things look to his eyes, and that she understands and respects his point of view. He will thus be helped to acknowledge his own emotions, and to sort out his attitude towards the girl and their child. It is often with a tremendous sense of relief that he finds himself able to talk about their relationship to someone who is sympathetic but unbiased. Presently his plans for the future will come to consideration. In the first place, does he wish to go on seeing the girl? This may appear a simple question, but it can be quite otherwise. What if he says 'No,' but – as often happens – the girl is still in love with him and wants to continue the relationship? Or the reverse, as in Alec's case, when the girl has withdrawn completely? Since love and hate are two sides of the same coin, the caseworker needs insight into the motivations of the people concerned, but even so it is often very difficult to get the partner who wants to continue the alliance to accept that without mutual willingness there can be no relationship at all.

What if the man is not free to marry, but declines to give up the girl? Here is one of the moral problems that beset social workers with unmarried parents. They, as representatives of society, are committed to upholding the institution of marriage; but what if the marriage is loveless beyond hope of revival? This is the familiar ground of all discussions on divorce, and outside the scope of this book. All that can be said here is that the social worker must assess every situation on its merits and relate her principles to it as best she can. She may find herself with a clear duty to use her influence to end the relationship between the parents and to rebuild the marriage, as with George and Eleanor (p. 53).

Next, can the young man help the girl, not only financially but emotionally, during the crisis? Practically all Mother and Baby Homes now allow the father to visit, and it has been found that, as with Tim and Cynthia at the beginning of this chapter, the fact of parenthood is immensely impressive to young people. Even if the relationship is not intended to be a permanent one, the father and mother can support each other during the crisis period, and he should feel himself involved in the decision about the child's future whenever possible. Now that he has a legal right to be heard in adoption proceedings it is more than ever important that he should be encouraged to participate as far as he can, and that his views should be known and acknowledged from an early stage.

Surprisingly often the unmarried father will ask wistfully 'Can I see the baby?' in a tone of voice which implies that he expects to be refused. What valid reason is there for denying him the sight of his own child? He will be much more willing to maintain his son or daughter if he is able to take an interest in the child's welfare, and the mother should be helped to agree to this whenever possible.

Once the father is sure of the worker's concern for him as a person, the question of his financial liability can be discussed with much less rancour. It must be clearly explained to him that any payment he makes to the mother will be regarded as proof of his responsibility for paternity, if in due course she applies to the court for an affiliation order. Similarly, should the child be adopted, his consent will be required if he has contributed to the infant's maintenance. The advantages and disadvantages of affiliation orders and private agreements, as described in the chapter on Keeping the Baby, can be discussed quite objectively, without committing the father. He will probably want to know what happens in the court, and here the caseworker is in a position to show him that the proceedings will be much simpler and more dignified if he admits his responsibility. Then, instead of the mother having to produce proof of his paternity, which may include love-letters and other intimate details, the magistrates have only to decide how much he is to pay. He can simplify matters even further by making an offer of a specific amount.

Much attention has been focused in the last few years on schoolgirl mothers, but schoolboy fathers have received far less consideration. No information is available as to their numbers, but the total is certainly quite considerable. Fred Smith has made a plea for better service for these young men. 'Only four out of a sample of fifty schoolboy fathers,' he says, 'had merely casual relationships with their girl-friends, and two-thirds had believed themselves to be in love.'[10] Here, surely, is a great need for skilled casework. Their parents also are often extremely troubled about the situation but do not know where to turn for help. This is pre-eminently a field for men caseworkers, but their absence should not be used by women as an excuse for opting out where help is needed.

To sum up, putative fathers are human beings and ought to be treated as such, not just as sources of money. The coming of the child is important to them, although they may react in different ways. Their difficulties are too seldom realised, but if given the opportunity they can make a great contribution to the well-being of mother and child, and it is well that they should do so.

4. The Social Worker

Many pregnant girls seem to solve their own problems without assistance from outside their family. Of the 67,056 illegitimate maternities in 1966, some 24,203 were referred to the various diocesan social work organisations, still best known as Moral Welfare Councils, whose work is co-ordinated by a committee of the Church Assembly's Board for Social Responsibility, and whose workers maintain the principal existing casework service for unmarried parents and their children. There is no means of knowing how many clients were helped by other agencies, including the Salvation Army, the National Council for the Unmarried Mother and Her Child, Medical Social Workers, the Probation Service and the Children's Departments, but even assuming that an equal number were in touch with them, there still remain 18,650 apparently not receiving casework help.

There are several reasons for this. Virginia Wimperis, referring to the Midboro study carried out in 1950, shows that no fewer than 39 per cent of the unmarried mothers in this town were sharing a home in stable union with the fathers of their children.[1] The Health Visitor who calls on such families in the course of her duties may become aware that there is no marriage certificate in the house, but so long as the cohabitation remains on a firm footing there will be no 'presenting problem' with regard to the child's care and keep, and therefore no reason for putting the mother in touch with a caseworker. Other women may be assumed to have married the father after the birth of their child. Again, there are many homes in which, although they always seem to be overcrowded already, the little 'by-blow' is made entirely welcome, and at once absorbed into the family as a full member with equal rights to whatever is going. A few unmarried mothers may just not have known where to turn for help, and some, especially the more intelligent, the older women and those of the professional classes, may simply prefer to cope with their own difficulties for themselves. At the other extreme, those who have been in conflict with the law, including many prostitutes, will avoid the caseworker as far as they can. In parts of rural Wales and Scotland, it used to be the custom for pregnancy to precede marriage, for economic reasons, because children were needed to help on the farm. If this still obtains, it is unlikely to swell the illegitimacy figures because the wedding would usually take place before the child was born. There is seldom any need for a caseworker in this situation. Moreover, it is well known that an indeterminate number of girls who conceive illegitimately will seek the help of an abortionist rather than continue with the pregnancy.

Hence it is clear that by no means all unmarried mothers are in touch with a caseworker, since many either do not want or do not need specialised help. Wimperis states that about 40 per cent of all the natural mothers in Midboro had some contact with a social worker. All the same, it is becoming increasingly clear that the existing casework service is patchy and inadequate. The evidence of the Association of Child Care Officers to the Seebohm Committee states bluntly that 'the family service should provide help for all unmarried mothers who would then have a casework service available as an alternative to an organisation which has a religious backing and a strong element of morality. . . . There is an urgent need for a more enlightened casework service to be made available to these mothers and their families.' Research such as Iris Goodacre's[2] has uncovered a great unmet need for skilled help on a long-term basis to be available not only to unmarried parents during the crisis period but to their children throughout adolescence and also to those who adopt them. There should be more specialist social workers available in every area to provide a single and continuous casework relationship for every client. This is of the first importance, because so many pregnant girls can only be effectually helped by strong support from someone whom they can regard as a second mother. This worker will remain in touch throughout her client's necessarily brief encounters with a succession of helpers: medical social workers, health visitors and nurses, doctors, adoption workers, Supplementary Benefits Commission officials and many others. A team of people is responsible for her care. The team needs a leader to guide the client and co-ordinate what is done for her. 'It's a good thing there are people like you. I never knew there were, before,' is a remark often made by clients to caseworkers. What sort of person should such a worker be, and what sort of equipment, in knowledge and in material resources and facilities, does she need?

The worker's personality

Essentially, she should have the personal qualities common to all good caseworkers. Much has been written about these in social work textbooks, and Helen Harris Perlman remarks that an account of all the caseworker must do and be makes her sound 'almost superhuman, an Olympian in mufti. But,' she goes on, 'the fact is that the caseworker too is only a human being, subject, like his client, to feelings of vanity, dislike, lovingness and vulnerability.'[3]

The caseworker's mainspring is a liking and concern for other people, just as they are; and this liking and concern motivates a wish to serve them which is sincere enough to include a willingness both to know and discipline herself, and to acquire by training and experience the ability to offer a professional service. Specifically, the specialist in problems of illegitimacy must have a liking and concern for unmarried parents. This implies a degree of maturity; she must have accepted the fact of sexuality both for herself and for others, and she should have come to terms with her own personal and particular sexual situation, whatever it may be. She must be perfectly clear and honest with herself about her own motives for dealing with this kind of difficulty. It is perhaps true that in the past too many 'good' women set out to rescue the fallen because their own sexual life was non-existent or unhappy, so that the lives and histories of 'bad' girls held a morbid fascination for them; they tended to react either with a harsh, punitive attitude which forfended all possibility of human understanding, or with a sentimentality equally unrealistic. Better knowledge of the dynamics of personality and greater skill in selecting prospective workers should now result in fewer misfits. It may be true, as some psychologists say, that in any case all social workers are motivated by 'sublimated voyeurism'. If so, let it be so. The important thing is that we should acknowledge the sexual element in our lives, be aware of it and use it constructively. The caseworker who has had a traumatic experience in childhood or adolescence can ultimately be the better for it if, instead of allowing it to fill her with anxiety and guilt, she uses it to gain insight. Indeed, there is no reason why a woman who has herself undergone the experience of unmarried motherhood should not make a first-rate caseworker, provided that she has truly outlived the experience and grown through it into greater maturity and understanding. As far as personal qualifications go, there is everything to be said for happily married wives and mothers engaging in this work.

Besides accepting her sexual experiences, whatever they may have been, the worker must also come to terms with her own emotions and prejudices. She will discover very early in her training that she has all sorts of affinities and aversions: that she warms naturally to the cheerful chatterbox who describes her relations with her boy-friend with unabashed impudence, but feels frustrated by the weeping individual who has absolutely nothing to say. She may find herself recoiling in active dislike from a girl whose pregnancy has wrecked a marriage, or coming into head-on collision with a militant mother who 'knows best' about her browbeaten daughter. Wise supervision during training will help her to build up an awareness of these innate tendencies, and so to modify them to some extent. Even more important, she will develop a habit of watchfulness towards her own reactions whenever she is face to face with a client.

'What the worker proves to be as a person often matters far more to clients than anything she may try to do on their behalf. In considering this subject it would seem that personal integrity, with all that it implies of frankness and straightforwardness in meeting and dealing with people, is a quality that must be reflected in every aspect of her work, difficult as it may be from time to time to meet helpfully the demands imposed by truthfulness and honesty. It would seem, too, that work with people who are in need or distress must always be undertaken in a spirit of humility. . . . But perhaps the most valuable quality a worker can bring to her clients is that which springs from a mind at ease and harmonious within itself; a mind in which tension and strain are at a minimum because her own emotional difficulties have been resolved or modified so that the problems of clients can be met in an unprejudiced way. It is this which constitutes the helping and healing element in relationships with people.'[4]

This quotation, although it is intended to apply to all caseworkers, could well have been written with those concerned with illegitimacy especially in mind. 'What the worker proves to be as a person' is often of crucial importance to a girl or young man whose opportunities, and, therefore, developed capacity, for relationships are limited. Indeed, the foundation of the whole helping process lies in the encounter between worker and client as people; more will be said of this in the next chapter. 'Integrity' is essential in one who must often walk in areas of acute moral difficulty, among such issues as contraception for the single, abortion, divorce and remarriage; who, moreover, will daily be confronted with questions of conflict and confidence as between parents and children, husbands and wives.

'Humility' is likely to be strengthened from day to day in workers who are receptive to what their clients can teach them. The first visit on a rainy morning, for instance, may be to a damp and stuffy basement flat, where the light is always on in the living-room. In these discouraging circumstances Mrs Ashton is doing the family washing with no amenities but the tin kettle on the gas stove. Her unemployed husband is hanging about, and five children keep getting under her feet. But Mrs Ashton is patient with the children, courteous to her husband, friendly to her visitor and always hopeful. 'How *does* she do it?' muses the worker as she goes on her way, and is jerked out of her Monday depression.

Iris, at the age of thirty-five, was living at home and looking after her elderly father when she fell in love with a divorced man. She fought hard to extricate herself, for divorce was contrary to her religious convictions and unchastity unthinkable. Yet it happened. Her shame and distress set the worker thinking, not 'There but for the grace of God go I', but in H. E. Williams' more profound phrase: 'There by the grace of God I have been, and am.'[5]

Humility will induce in the worker a readiness to admit mistakes, and to co-operate with others. It will also motivate a lifelong willingness to increase her knowledge and improve her skill, so that she may be more effectual as a helping person.

All social workers, and perhaps especially those who are concerned with unmarried parenthood, are from time to time confronted by their clients with some of the most difficult questions about life and death. 'There can't be a God, or he wouldn't have let this happen' is an attitude that often has to be faced. 'What have I done to deserve this?' cries the anguished father of a pregnant girl. 'God won't love me now – I shall go to hell,' sobs the frightened fifteen-year-old newly discovered to be pregnant. These are often appeals for help. How can the worker respond effectively? She cannot simply opt out in the critical moment of her client's distress. To say 'You'd better talk about that with a clergyman' would be intolerable, even though this is certainly the area of pastoral care rather than casework. In this situation all the worker's human warmth and sympathy, and all the skill and insight she has acquired by training, are not enough by themselves. She cannot offer any real answer to the client's question unless she has a faith or philosophy of her own. The writer of this book is convinced that Christianity offers by far the most perceptive approach to the mysteries of good and evil; moreover it identifies the source of the compassion which, as Professor Halmos says, motivates the 'counsellors' of today.

Her training

The personal qualities desirable in a caseworker helping unmarried parents are, then, in the first place a liking for people and a wish to serve them; secondly, acceptance of her whole self; and integrity, humility and faith. Finally, it is well if all this excellence is rounded off with common sense and a sense of humour. What of the training, knowledge and experience that will equip her as a professional helping person?

Ideally, the foundation should be a recognised course of social science. Almost all universities now run two-year diploma and three-year degree courses, which offer the necessary knowledge of contemporary society and the workings of the Welfare State. An alternative qualification would be a Certificate in Social Work from a College of Further Education, or a Letter of Recognition in Child Care from a two-year non-academic Home Office course. Practical work placements during training will be widely varied, but will probably include periods with a Children's Department, a Family Service Unit or the National Society for the Prevention of Cruelty to Children to give insight into the various crises that can occur in family life. (It is hoped that the student can draw upon her own childhood and upbringing for knowledge of what 'ordinary' domestic life is like.) The basic course, whatever its nature, should be followed by a period of specialised training, which will include further study of psychology and ethics. Josephine Butler College, Liverpool, offers courses of this kind, and also shorter periods of training specially adapted for older women with relevant experience who wish to work with natural parents.

Experience with babies and young children is a very valuable asset, for the worker who is helping unmarried parents should be able to assess the progress of the child. Not only should she be familiar with the signs of neglect or wrong treatment, but it helps her contact with her client if she is able to offer practical suggestions about small daily problems, and an over-anxious mother can be greatly reassured if the worker who has called to see her can handle a fretful baby with competence. A well-run day nursery, nursery school or children's hospital may provide practice of this kind.

The student will, in addition to her knowledge of social administration in general, need to become very familiar with the workings of the Ministry of Social Security, for the great majority of her clients will apply for maternity grants and allowances, and many will be on sick pay or supplementary benefits. She should therefore have a working knowledge of the scales of payment, qualifying conditions and methods of application for these, and moreover should understand something of the organisation of the Ministry and its local offices.

Psychology is a vital part of the worker's theoretical equipment. 'A knowledge of the science of human relations,' says Biestek, 'is necessary because the caseworker deals intimately with people. . . . The knowledge of how human personality grows, changes, reacts to life's stresses, normally and abnormally, serves as a framework in which the individual client is better understood.'[6] Field workers may find themselves unable to accept some of the more abstruse theories of Freudian and Kleinian psychology, but its essential statements have transformed our understanding of how people act and react on one another. In particular, the specialist in illegitimacy should have as full a knowledge as she can acquire of the psychology of sexuality, childhood and maternity. This will give her insight into her clients that she could never attain by her own 'hunches', however perceptive she may be.

The client, moreover, never exists in isolation. The pregnant girl not only has a boy-friend – or more than one – but also parents, brothers and sisters, school friends or workmates, and with all these people she lives in a multiplicity of relationships. Without them, she could not be herself at all. Hence the growing interest of social workers in the theory of group dynamics, which can make a further contribution to our understanding of the origin and nature of the problem. The full possibilities of group therapy are still not explored, but in suitable conditions it can offer a fruitful alternative to casework with individuals.

The caseworker concerned with illegitimacy will find herself confronted with moral and ethical problems of great complexity from time to time. To give some common examples, she may know, for instance, that Elsie is cheating the Ministry of Social Security by earning £5 a week at a part-time job, as well as drawing her allowance. What ought she to do about this? How much should prospective adopters be told about a child suspected of being born of incest? Or Greta admits to the worker that she has lied to her parents about the father of her baby. The worker will also have to make difficult decisions of policy with regard to her client, particularly concerning the use of available resources and where the claims of one client upon her time, energy and skill conflict with those of others. In order to help her to think clearly and logically through these dilemmas, it is very desirable that she should have some understanding of ethical principles as they stand today, and some practice during training in applying these to the complications of daily living.[7]

It may be added that if she wishes to remain fully effective as a caseworker, the specialist must beware of strangulation by her own speciality. It is surprisingly easy to become so absorbed in illegitimacy as to forget that there are many millions of ordinary, happy young people who marry first and have children afterwards; or, more subtly, to assume that her highly technical approach to the relationships between men and women is the only possible one. An effective way of remaining human is to read contemporary fiction. Novels like Alan Sillitoe's *Saturday Night and Sunday Morning* or Stan Barstow's *A Kind of Loving* will help to correct the clinical attitude, and keep her in touch with the daily lives of ordinary people.

A crucial part of the worker's training is the first three years of her first appointment. In the past, too many newly qualified women were placed in isolated areas where they were obliged to work on their own, so that they had very inadequate opportunities for consultation with more experienced workers. This imposed unjustifiable strain upon them, and led not only to some unnecessary and disastrous blunders which experience could have avoided, but also to the formation of habits and methods of working which were not always of the best, and moreover were difficult to correct. The newly qualified worker will probably benefit most if she is regarded as a junior member of a team, so that she has plenty of opportunity for discussion with colleagues. She needs guidance and support as she first shoulders responsibility in situations which are often both complex and distressing.

The agency and administration

'The recognition of . . . various social problems, such as unmarried parenthood, does not imply that a special "field" must be created to handle it, but that special aptitudes and knowledge are called for,' says Gordon Hamilton, stressing the importance to all branches of social work of their 'common philosophy and techniques'.[8] Nevertheless, as Noel Timms points out, 'casework does not begin with a relationship, but with a worker and a client meeting in a particular kind of social agency'.[9] What 'particular kind of social agency' will make the best framework for the 'special aptitudes and knowledge' needed for casework with unmarried parents?

In *The Church in Social Work* Hall and Howes have given a detailed and lucid account of the way in which the existing diocesan casework services developed. The main preoccupation of the reformers of the last century was with the rescue of 'fallen women', and the immediate need was to get them off the streets; 'shelters' and 'refuges' were opened throughout the country, and staffed by women whose 'self-devotion' was the only qualification asked of them. It was not until the end of the century that the need for specific training was recognised, and Mrs Ruspini began to run courses for students at St Agnes House, London, in 1898. At this time, interest still focused on 'indoor work'. The appointment of the first 'outdoor workers', who were the forerunners of the present-day caseworkers, is not well recorded. In early days the Superintendent of a Shelter did a certain amount of visiting of girls in their own homes in her area, and Miss J. E. Higson, who started a training school at St Monica's Refuge, Liverpool, in 1911, sent her students out on visits, but it seems likely that the appointment of full-time caseworkers, not attached to any Shelter or Home, became more widespread during the First World War. After the opening of Josephine Butler Memorial House, as it then was, in 1920, a small but steady supply of trained workers became available, and Moral Welfare Associations up and down the country began to employ them.

The organisation of the work done could hardly have been more haphazard. Each association was started by local people concerned with local needs, and in due course Organising Secretaries were appointed by the dioceses to co-ordinate the work of perhaps half a dozen such local organisations, which were then affiliated to a diocesan Moral Welfare Council. In many places the local units have now merged into a single diocesan body, which provides a more consistent service. Lack of funds is still a problem almost everywhere, in spite of varying degrees of help from Local Authorities. In 1932 the Church of England Advisory Board for Moral Welfare Work was established, but despite various changes of title and status the function of its present-day successor, the Committee for Diocesan Moral and Social Welfare Councils of the Church Assembly Board for Social Responsibility, is still to advise and co-ordinate the work of the autonomous dioceses and local committees, and there is as yet no central direction of the available workers.

The present-day Church social worker, therefore, is employed either by a diocesan council or a local association, which will define its aims and objects in some such terms as these:

'To help: 1. Young people in trouble, loneliness or moral danger,
2. Unmarried parents and their children,
3. Married couples drifting apart,
4. Parents in perplexity about their children,
5. Educational and preventive work.'

She will be required to report to a case committee, composed of clergy and lay people whose interest and knowledgeability will vary between the two extremes, and she will also have a diocesan organising secretary, usually a mature and experienced worker to whom she can turn for guidance. Her relations with her local authority colleagues will be conditioned by the siting of her office, which may or may not be convenient for easy collaboration, and by the boundaries of her district which, as it is based upon Anglican deaneries, is unlikely to coincide with Local Authority areas. For this reason one worker may find herself with as many as three or more different sets of colleagues in separate Children's Departments, Welfare Departments and Social Security areas. Hence the quality of her administrative arrangements may vary from the very, very good to the horrid, depending entirely upon the chances of human personality and geography.

The church worker may find herself involved in a conflict of loyalties at least as often as her colleague in the statutory services. Like her, she has a duty to society as well as to her client, and, in addition, has to reconcile her commitment to the church as an institution with the standards of the secular world – often an extremely difficult matter. Similarly, the Local Authority worker owes allegiance to her department. Nevertheless, the Church worker's stance outside the statutory social work organisations has some very great advantages. Because she is not in any sense an official, her relationship with her client is based upon free and willing acceptance of her as a helping person, and her authority is based simply upon her professional competence. The fact that Mrs White – that neurotic woman – is perfectly free never to come near the worker's office again is the greatest possible help in maintaining a relationship with her, and in this Mrs White is in a very different position from a probationer or the parents of a child in care. The voluntary worker also has freedom from red tape in regard to hours and methods of work, and her committee is free to experiment at her suggestion if she sees new needs or fresh possibilities.

The statutory services, on the other hand, have greater resources at their disposal, and their workers are therefore less likely to be overworked and underpaid. Because they operate on a larger scale, they can be so organised as to make the best possible use of the people available, and their structure both depends on and enables good communications. The challenge of the immediate future is to find some means of preserving the spontaneity of a voluntary service in a larger, more uniform, organisation. For example, it is essential in casework of a very personal nature that the worker in touch with a client must sign her own letters. She must be free to be unconventional in her hours of work and methods of helping; if Mrs White refuses to go away on holiday because she cannot afford to send her dog to the kennels, an allowance must be forthcoming; if the best way to have a talk with a putative father is to meet him at a transport café at 3 a.m., the worker must be free to do so – and not be compelled by regulations to arrive at the office at 9 o'clock next morning.

The need for a single casework relationship

The greatest need where unmarried parents are concerned is for continuity of casework. The relation between client and worker is the most important of all the means of help, and the sooner in her pregnancy the single girl is referred, the stronger this relationship will become. 'The need to build this relationship during the pregnancy is vividly demonstrated by the extreme difficulty of working with a girl who has had no casework help before delivery and then has to face her problems all at once and without the safe anchor of a supporting relationship.'[10] The caseworker will go with the girl to the Mother and Baby Home, visit her during her stay there, help her to plan for the future and support her during the subsequent months whether she parts with the baby or keeps him; and the same worker will also help the putative father as far as possible. It is no doubt unavoidable that the girl will be seen by many others, including the medical social worker and perhaps a representative of the adoption society, but if she has her own worker to act as a mother-figure throughout, the casework done is incomparably better than if she has been handed from one 'helper' to another in a process which feels to her about as personal as a sausage machine. Alexina McWhinnie has recently stressed the importance of this comprehensive casework approach, not only from the mother's point of view, but also as being of fundamental importance in planning the adoption of her child.[11] Administrative arrangements must therefore be designed to foster this continuity, by ensuring speedy referral to the specialist worker and by allowing her enough freedom of action to deal with each case as it develops. Also, for two reasons there should be no deadline for closing a case. Unmarried mothers are often inadequate people who are neither physically nor mentally equipped to make their own way in life, and the worker who sees them through the initial crisis may still be needed years afterwards as a barrier against despair and emptiness. Furthermore, as Jane Rowe points out, there is a whole field of casework largely untouched among growing children, whether illegitimate or adopted, who are troubled about their origin, and among adoptive parents. The caseworker who remains in touch, or at least accessible, can often prevent small problems from growing into big ones.

This has implications for the length of time the worker should stay in her job. Real continuity is obviously impossible if she moves every three years; once she has gained experience, ten or twelve years in one place will not be too long. When the time comes for her to go, the inevitable transfers must be arranged with care and forethought, so that Mrs White has a chance to work through her conviction that she 'won't like the new woman'.

In view of the present shortage of all kinds of social workers, it is perhaps unrealistic to discuss the size of the caseload. But both the specialist worker herself and those administratively responsible for her must see that she is not overburdened with routine duties, and that her car, typewriter and dictating machine are reasonably new and perfectly efficient. With these aids, she should be able to do good casework with a maximum annual intake of 100–120 new cases per year, and a current caseload of 50–80. A large proportion of workers at the present time carry much higher numbers than this, but too many on the books inevitably means hurried, superficial interviewing, and intensive individual casework becomes impossible.

'Today the trend is towards a responsible alignment of structures and functions in an overall community plan of welfare,' wrote Gordon Hamilton in 1940, referring to the United States.[12] In Great Britain this ideal may shortly come nearer to realisation. There is much to be said in favour of a single service for all unsupported mothers – widows, divorced and deserted wives as well as unmarried girls. In particular, such a service would greatly help to lessen the stigma of illegitimacy, which is perhaps reinforced as long as natural children are in a category by themselves.

Whatever the administrative setting and however it may change in the future, the need for co-operation with other agencies will remain important. Teamwork within the agency itself needs to be paralleled by teamwork among all the social workers in the area. In the past it has been unusual for any practising caseworker to see all the social provisions of her district as a unified service to the public; indeed they were not so at all, but consisted of a multiplicity of independent services run by independent bodies, with little administrative co-ordination between them. Hence the worker in one department felt herself to be in competition with those in another department, even within the same Local Authority, and those employed by voluntary bodies, perhaps because they were usually paid much less, tended to imagine themselves looked down upon by Local Authority workers. Given these conditions, the classical case in which sixteen social workers were visiting one family independently is understandable enough. Co-operation has depended too much upon the personal qualities of individual workers. It is greatly to be hoped that unification of the social services will not only lessen the competition between departments but also provide a workable system of co-operation among them.

The worker responsible for the care of natural parents and their children will find herself especially closely in touch with Medical Social

Workers and Child Care Officers, the Medical Officer of Health, Health Visitors and doctors, voluntary bodies such as Dr Barnardo's Homes and the Children's Society, and perhaps also with an independent adoption agency. She should make it her business to know personally the workers and officials concerned, as far as possible, maintaining a working relationship of trust and confidence with them, and also to make administrative arrangements that will help communication. In particular, they should know exactly when she will be in her office and available for consultation by telephone or in person, and nothing short of major emergencies should prevent her from being there at the time stated. Care in passing on relevant information and keeping colleagues in touch is not only courteous, but so lubricates the machinery of the organisation that its working efficiency is vastly improved.

Since the preceding paragraphs were written, the Seebohm Report has appeared. It proposes a unified social service department especially designed to promote close co-operation, and recommends that the same social worker should handle all the problems relating to a single individual or family. The paragraph relating to unmarried mothers reads:

> The risks to which the young illegitimate child is exposed are greater than those faced by legitimate children and they are likely to need more help from the social service department. Likewise unmarried mothers also need special assistance. Where they retain their children and look after them, help is necessary in the form of guidance, accommodation and in ensuring adequate income. We recognise the outstanding pioneering work which has been done by voluntary bodies in this field, particularly religious organisations, and there is no suggestion that they be superseded. But we do recommend that, first, there should be a realistic alternative source of assistance to those unmarried mothers who do not wish to approach religious bodies and, second, that there should be a clear assignment of responsibility to the social service department for ensuring adequate social care and advice for both the unmarried mother and her child.[13]

This proposal is most welcome. It is right that the parents of illegitimate children should not be compelled to approach a religious agency simply because there is no alternative. Individual dioceses are free to make their own arrangements with the Local Authorities according to local conditions. The need for lively and adventurous voluntary organisations is specifically mentioned in the Report, and the way is now clear for diocesan councils to experiment, perhaps with new kinds of homes and hostels to meet new needs, perhaps with new casework methods, perhaps with projects for community care. Moreover there will be many opportunities for the present Church social workers to co-operate with Local Authorities in setting up a new service, because their knowledge and experience in dealing with illegitimacy is unique.

The sources from which cases are referred to the worker vary to some extent, but in most areas the majority come from Medical Social Workers, Children's Officers and general practitioners. The pregnant girl's first action is very often to go to see her own doctor, who, according to his judgment of the whole situation, may refer her for help, perhaps with a view to her admission to a Mother and Baby Home. If the girl wishes to be confined at home or in the local hospital, she is likely to be interviewed by the Medical Social Worker at the ante-natal clinic, and she in her turn, if she sees possible difficulties, may contact the specialist worker. A certain proportion of referrals come from clergy, others from schools. It is not unusual for a former client to bring her sister, or a friend who has asked her help. A mother whose son has been before the Court may ask the Probation Officer's advice about her pregnant daughter, and be referred to the worker concerned. Finally, the girl who cannot bring herself to confide in anyone at home, but writes in desperation to the 'problem page' of a woman's magazine, receives in reply a note from the National Council for the Unmarried Mother and Her Child, giving her the name of her local worker, to whom she may write or telephone.

By all these ways, the clients come to the worker's door. What happens when they meet?

5. The First Interview

The first meeting between the caseworker and a new client is of crucial importance, because it moulds the whole future relationship between them, and this relationship, as has already been shown, is the principal tool in helping unmarried parents. Mistakes by the worker at this stage will not only hamper progress, but can in fact do great harm if the client goes away disappointed and unsatisfied, for she will probably not return and so perhaps never receive the help she may greatly need.

The complicated processes that begin when caseworker and client first confront one another go on simultaneously on two levels, the practical and the psychological. Both are important, and both are closely and subtly linked together.

Reception

The client already has an impression of the agency before she reaches its door, for an appointment has usually been made before the interview takes place. Was the voice that answered the telephone friendly, interested but not fussy, and clear? Was the letter well typed, in simple language, and explicit?

Dear Miss Jones,

Dr Robinson has given me your name and address and asked me to get in touch with you. I am very sorry to hear of your problem, and will certainly do anything I can to help.

I understand you are free on Thursday afternoons, and so I am wondering whether it will be convenient for you to come to my office on Thursday next, 8th July, at 3 p.m. If this does not suit you, perhaps you would get in touch with me and we can arrange another date.

The office is quite easy to find. It is on the first floor above Smith's shoe shop, nearly at the bottom of High Street.

Yours sincerely,

In spite of encouragement, however, the pregnant girl nearly always approaches the agency in a state of apprehension. It is no light matter to put oneself into the hands of a complete stranger in a situation so personal and so embarrassing; indeed her approach to the caseworker is at this stage a great extra cause of anxiety, another problem to contend with. Her mingled dread of the unknown and hope of getting help render her highly sensitive to new impressions. This is why it is important that the agency's premises should contrive to combine a welcoming human atmosphere with orderliness and efficiency. There should be colour and light, flowers and comfortable chairs as well as the inevitable telephone, typewriters and filing cabinets. Cardboard cartons full of second-hand toys and clothing are much better stowed in cupboards out of sight, and empty coffee-cups do not add grace to the clutter on the desk. Top-coats and well-filled shopping baskets should not be on view to invite the client to compare the caseworker's standard of living with her own. She should not be kept waiting if it can be avoided.

Things begin to happen in the first moment in which client and caseworker confront one another. Both receive and rapidly sort their first impressions, and react in accordance with them. In the first few minutes the client should be able to modify some of her negative feelings and arrive at a more responsive attitude: 'She's quite old, really,' she may think, facing the worker, 'but at least she isn't sarcastic. And she's not going to tell me off. I can talk to this person.' How does she get these impressions? The look in the eyes, the movement of the hands, the courtesy with which she is received and offered a comfortable chair will convey to her the thing she needs to know: that here is a woman who not only understands her situation and is skilled in dealing with it, but who also is interested in her as a person and is prepared to listen to what she has to say. The experienced worker will be quite aware of this reaction, and she herself will be simultaneously learning the identity of her client in the same manner. The girl's appearance and bearing tell her a great deal; her dress will give some indication not only of her social standing but of her personality and temperament also. The client may be slovenly and careless of her looks, or the reverse; why is this? The worker already begins to analyse her impressions as well as to receive them. Is it poverty, upbringing, narcissism or the sheer weight of her troubles that have made her as she is? The hands, the eyes, the set of the mouth tell her a great deal about this person who has come to see her. But if the caseworker is wise she does not therefore assume that she 'knows' her client from this first confrontation; some caseworkers seem to pride themselves on their ability to sum people up at a glance, but this is a pitfall. First impressions are always valuable, but they will need to be amplified, sifted and perhaps greatly modified as the relationship develops.

Client and caseworker will sit not with a desk as a barrier between them, preferably not face to face as this may discomfit the client if she feels she cannot escape the caseworker's eyes, but at an oblique angle to one another, and light should fall upon the client's face but without causing her discomfort. She should be encouraged to smoke if she wants to. Interruptions should be kept to a minimum; if the telephone rings the caseworker will arrange to call back the enquirer whenever possible, and return to her client with an apology: 'I'm sorry about that. You were saying . . .' And however great the pressure upon her she will not allow the client to get the impression that she has no time for her. If she cannot spare half an hour for someone who has called without an appointment, she can show interest and concern in making a date for an interview shortly afterwards. Even so, pregnant girls, and their mothers, are quite liable to come hot-foot from the doctor's surgery with a very urgent and immediate need to talk, and the experienced caseworker, recognising this, will be prepared to delay her round of visits in order to listen if it is really necessary.

Attitudes and approaches

At this point it is as well to be clear about what the client has come for. The girl herself is very unlikely to be able to say exactly what she hopes for or expects from the agency – supposing that the caseworker asked her, although in fact she seldom does this. A notable exception was a persuasive little woman who said: 'Now I'll tell you what I want you to do for us, Miss P. I just want you to arrange for our Edna to go into one of these convents. I know there are such places, and she won't have to see the baby at all and she can come right home. You can do that for us, can't you?' Far more often the girl, and her more articulate mother, know only that they have been told that this 'welfare woman' will help them, and because they feel overwhelmed by the situation they come to see what she can do. It may be that the girl already has some idea of whether she intends to keep her baby or to offer him for adoption; in the former case she will perhaps look for advice about how to obtain an affiliation order, and in the latter for guidance as to how to go about adoption. She may also be wondering about National Insurance maternity benefits. She may be anxious to go away and hide, or perhaps want to find the putative father who has disappeared. Her problem is always a complex one, and sometimes one aspect of it is uppermost and sometimes another. But at this stage it is the practical considerations that ask to be dealt with first, and the client comes for help with these rather than their emotional undertones. She seldom realises, until she and the caseworker have begun to work together on the situation, that the practical problems cannot be isolated from how she feels about them, and that indeed her emotions may be the worst part of the difficulty. Some clients seem to clutch at the caseworker like a drowning man at a plank, others are overwhelmed with diffidence at having to ask for help, some feel it necessary to try to save some shreds of their self-respect by being as remote and detached as possible, and constantly apologise for 'troubling' the worker.

She for her part can bring to the encounter the knowledge and skill to cope with the practical difficulties, but she is much more aware than her client of the implications of the total situation, and furthermore her training has given her some degree of psychological insight into the most effectual methods of helping. She knows, therefore, that she must start where the client is. This means that in the first place, through her natural perceptiveness and her acquired knowledge, she must gain a realistic understanding of the girl in front of her. Superficially, Mary is a bottle-blonde aged twenty-five who is expecting a baby in three months' time; but the worker, as she pieces her story together, will perceive that she is so carefully got-up because she feels insecure, and this insecurity has its origin in the events leading up to her parents' divorce when she was six years old. Further knowledge of facts, and even the most fleeting impressions gained from her manner and tone of voice, as well as what she says or does not say, will add relevant detail to the picture: that the client has an emotional block where children are concerned, and that her fantasy-self is a television personality rather than a wife and mother. She loves dancing, but seldom goes to the cinema because she 'cries too much at the sad parts'. The apologetic smile with which she says this shows that she is to some extent aware of her own immaturity.

This understanding of her client, this getting alongside her in order to start where she is, is in no sense a coldly analytical process, even though it requires a certain detachment, and skill and knowledge have a great deal to do with it. It is motivated and carried through by a warm human feeling, the liking and concern for people mentioned in the last chapter as the first essential of a good caseworker. Her faith in the incalculable value of the individual is not merely a subject of intellectual assent; she feels it in her blood and bones and it is apparent in her approach, however insignificant or unattractive her client may appear. The word 'empathy' is used to describe the social worker's capacity for entering right into the client's situation, bringing into it the understanding of its reality she has gained from her own objective viewpoint. From this arises the supportive healing attitude sometimes described as 'acceptance', which is in fact a very special kind of love, the love which 'knows all about you and loves you just the same'.

This acceptance of the client is the foundation of the casework relationship with unmarried parents. They so often feel cut off from the rest of humanity by their sense of guilt and worthlessness; in their isolation they are frightened, perhaps aggressive, perhaps withdrawn. But in either case their lifeline, their main hope of restoration to human fellowship, is a person who accepts them with a love which can look squarely at all that they are and all that they feel themselves to be, and not be withdrawn; a love which moreover has faith in the client's ability to put right what has gone wrong, and will offer help and support in the effort. Self-respect, in the sense that one is a good sort of person and worth something, has taken a toss; and to find oneself actually liked, loved and trusted in spite of all that has happened is a humbling and vitalising experience.

The caseworker must be able and willing to offer this experience to all her clients, even though in practice some will not want it in its fullness and some will be unable to receive it. Almost all, however, are sensitive to the caseworker's acceptance of them. The most nervous or self-absorbed client is aware when the caseworker is relaxed and friendly, and giving her her undivided attention.

The caseworker can do this only if her own mind is at peace; she must herself have experienced acceptance before she can offer it to others. Psychoanalysis, if it is constructively handled, can afford this to some people; to others it comes through religious faith, or from a deeply loving relationship with another person. In either case the result is release from preoccupation with oneself, and a fresh capacity for love of one's neighbour. But this is not achieved by any individual in isolation. Biestek[1] says that self-acceptance leads to acceptance of others, but in practice this is a two-way process, since it is in relationship with others that a person discovers himself. It could as well be said that acceptance of others leads to acceptance of oneself, while at the same time self-knowledge fosters empathy with other people.

Being, by whatever means, released from preoccupations with herself, the caseworker is free to give her whole attention to her client. This may well be a new experience for the pregnant girl or anxious parent, and therapeutic in itself. The overwrought person will be able to relax in her presence, and the aggressive one will find that there is no need for her to take the offensive because she is not going to be attacked.

But what, basically, will be the specialist caseworker's approach towards the unmarried mother? Many of her clients will have a lively sense that they have 'done wrong', and will expect to be punished in some way; hence their expectation that the social worker will be critical or 'tell them off'. She does not do so. She knows well that most of her clients are psychologically sick or emotionally starved, and that those who are neither the one nor the other are often the victims of hard circumstances. To sit in judgment is no part of a caseworker's job. This may sound as though there is no place in her philosophy for moral law, and indeed she has sometimes been accused of condoning immorality because she refuses to condemn her clients' conduct out of hand. Charges of 'helping bad girls to get worse' are sometimes made. Nothing could be further from the truth. The worker with unmarried parents has more reason than most people to acknowledge the necessity of the moral code, for she sees at first hand the tragic consequences of breaking it in terms of human suffering. But the service she provides is essentially a rescue operation, an ambulance service. She is there to unravel the causes and the motives of her clients' behaviour, with the sole purpose of enabling them to live more freely and more constructively in future. As a seasoned worker once said: 'I pick 'em up, brush 'em down and start 'em off on the right road.'

How does the caseworker convey to the client that although she in some degree understands the reasons for it, she nevertheless does not condone the immoral conduct? Probably not specifically in words, but in her whole approach to the situation. She will never regard the girl's problem lightly. The implicit acknowledgment that the client has broken the moral law will always be there and taken seriously as a factor in the whole situation, even though less time and attention will usually be given to it than is spent on positive and constructive plans for the future. If the client herself adopts a hard, couldn't-care-less or frivolous attitude the worker will be able to see, and communicate with, the underlying guilt and fear, and wherever guilt is present in a marked degree, the worker will look for appropriate means of release.

Much has been written about the non-judgmental attitude in casework textbooks,[2] yet there is still room for speculation as to whether it is always right to avoid overtly criticising the client's conduct. So many of them expect it. 'I think I ought to have been whipped, but everyone was so determined to be kind and understanding,' 'I'd have felt better if you'd given me a proper telling-off,' they say. Is the desire to suffer in return for wrongdoing mere masochism, or a healthy wish to even the score so as to be on equal terms with society again? No one would ever recommend that caseworkers should bend their clients over chairs and administer three swishes with the office ruler, but there are rare occasions when crisp and frank comments on their conduct have a bracing effect. These, however, belong to a later stage in the casework process.

Exploring the problem

To return to the first interview. No two ever develop in the same way. The caseworker is at the client's disposal, and it is best if the client lays the trail. She may play for time with an apology for lateness or a remark about the weather, or comment upon the gallery of babies' photographs above the mantelpiece. Recognitions and adjustments are being made all the time. One client may cover her discomfort with a pert air of detachment, but another appears so distressed as to be almost unaware of her surroundings, able only to stammer out the critical words, 'I'm going to have a baby'. Why is this? Is it that she is ashamed of having to come for help, or is she feeling guilty about her conduct, or remorseful now that it has been found out, or simply afraid of the consequences? Or a mixture of all these? The caseworker, accepting the situation as it is, encourages the release of the client's emotional tensions. Sometimes she has to let the pregnant girl go through an outburst of tears, sometimes to help by gentle questioning one who is tongue-tied by anxiety, and sometimes to contend with a torrent of incoherent speech. The emotional and psychological content of any personal problem is often its most important part, and this is particularly so in the case of an illegitimate pregnancy. The caseworker may find that her chief objective in the first interview is to help the girl to work out her own feelings of fear and shame.

However, it does not always happen that the emotional content of the situation must be ventilated first. Sometimes the client has a great deal of self-control, can outline her situation quite objectively and asks only for factual information about arrangements for her confinement. The caseworker will respond appropriately and make no attempt to probe at this stage, but she should be clear as to why her client is enquiring. A new client once asked straight away how to set about getting her baby adopted. The worker made a mistake; instead of asking why the information was wanted, she accepted the enquiry at its face value and began to answer it. As she proceeded she became convinced that she was 'off the client's wavelength', and presently the sister who accompanied her broke in with: 'But Betty, you haven't told the lady you don't *want* it adopted!' whereupon a fresh start had to be made.

It often happens that a young pregnant girl will come to the agency with her mother or a friend to give her moral support. In this case it is usually as well to see them both together, at any rate in the early part of the interview, partly because it would be unfair and unwise to deprive the girl of the comfort she wants and needs, but also because the supporter can help to give the caseworker a stereoscopic view of the situation. Later on, it is to be hoped that the girl will have developed enough confidence to see the worker alone and to talk freely with her. Mothers can be casework problems in themselves and need as much help, but their tendency to dominate the interview as they have dominated the lives of their daughters must be controlled. Sometimes one or both parents will come to the agency without their daughter in the first instance, as in the case of Alison (p. 41). This fact in itself tells a great deal about the family; obviously it is one in which the parents feel deeply involved in their daughter's situation, but the experienced worker will beware of assuming that they are therefore over-protective. Alison's parents had in fact allowed her a great deal of freedom, but in this crisis (the greatest they had ever had to face) they instlnctively drew together to protect her.

At the first interview the client will tell her story for herself in the first instance, with as much or as little prompting from the caseworker as she may need. As to the nature of the prompting, Perlman[3] usefully points out that questions usually direct themselves to the answerer's mind, and comments address themselves to her mood. It may be helpful to say: 'Tell me about your family; have you still got both parents?' but to ask 'Why did you feel like that?' usually flummoxes a client and sets her looking for logical reasons why she felt as she did. To encourage the client to talk about her feelings it is better to comment: 'I see. I don't expect you liked that,' or 'This certainly sounds like a problem.' As she listens, the worker is sorting and analysing what she is told, for the facts are not likely to come in an orderly progression, and in any case are of two kinds: the objective ones that she needs to fill in the front sheet of the casepaper (works at the mill, father a seaman, boy-friend an electrician) and the intangibles (didn't know he was married, jealous of her older sister). Sometimes there seem to be areas where the client shows hesitation because they are emotionally charged, especially where her relationship with the putative father is concerned. A caseworker who is herself sensitive and reticent may be inclined to skate over them, but this is a mistake. She will not be able to help her client unless there is complete openness between them, and she must not give the impression that here is something which she is unwilling to share, or which might arouse her disapproval. On the other hand she must never appear to be forcing confidences; it is often as well to do no more than make a mental note of the difficulties at this stage, and return to them at a later interview.

The caseworker gradually builds up a tentative outline of the situation and will begin to formulate ideas as to what steps might be taken to deal with it, but she has at the same time to evaluate the client's capacity for constructive action. The girl may put all the facts, as she sees them, before the caseworker and then ask: 'What can I do?' or she may stumble incoherently through her story with frequent expressions of inability to cope or to understand. Quite often she will, consciously or unconsciously, look to the caseworker as a supernaturally wise person who can produce some magic solution, and will wait for her good advice or clear-cut directions to this end. But the worker knows well that the only valid way is to help her client to help herself, and therefore her response at this point will depend very much on the assessment she has been able to make of the client's personality and capabilities. Is she intellectually and emotionally able to formulate a workable plan for herself, and has she enough determination to carry it out? The first step with the voluble and confused client is to break down her huge and nebulous problem into separate pieces of manageable size, select one or two for immediate action, and work through these to the others. This will help the girl to think clearly, and will encourage her to see that when faced in this way the situation is not as hopeless as it looks. The demand for advice is very often motivated by fear or guilt, and reflects a wish to unload responsibility on to the worker. In this case it is best to bring the fear into the open. Quite frequently the client, having asked a direct question: 'What do you think I should do?' goes on without a pause to propound a solution of her own; she merely hopes for the worker's support in what she proposes to do.

Working towards a solution

Elizabeth came with a ready-made scheme which the worker knew perfectly well to be quite impracticable: she would go to London, find a job and lodgings on the day of her arrival, get someone to place her baby for adoption and return home without telling her family anything about it. Instead of flatly insisting that this plan was unworkable, the caseworker discussed it objectively, and even helped the girl to make some genuine attempt to find the lodgings, in order to let her be convinced for herself that the scheme must be abandoned.

Unwillingness to tell the parents is often a major difficulty, and the first that has to be faced. Many girls, like Elizabeth, will try desperately to avoid it. There may be psychological reasons for this, particularly in the case of those who have been dominated by either father or mother, but in many emotionally well-balanced girls it seems to arise not merely from fear of their anger but from a perfectly genuine unwillingness to bring upon their parents the shock and distress they will inevitably feel. The worker will discuss ways and means; she can point out that nearly all parents, when at last they know the truth, are more distressed by the fact that their daughter could not confide in them than by the pregnancy itself. Elizabeth ultimately took a job in a neighbouring town, and told her mother when she first went to visit her there; Miss R., it will be remembered (p. 30), left her home and delayed writing to tell her parents. Kathleen (p. 34) left a letter on the kitchen table when she went to work, Margaret (p. 46) decided to tell her mother while they were cooking the Sunday dinner together.

The next question is very often 'Where will the baby be born?', but before this can be answered it is necessary to have some idea of what is planned for the child. If the mother has quite decided to keep her baby and there are no family difficulties in the way of this, there is no apparent reason why the confinement should not take place in the nearest maternity hospital; even so, it sometimes happens that the expectant mother prefers to be out of sight for the last few weeks of her confinement, and have expert help in managing the baby for a few weeks before she brings him home. If adoption is intended, or if his future is uncertain, then it is unrealistic to expect the mother to have the baby in her own home at any time, and then be able to send him away. Worker and client together will discuss the pros and cons of a Mother and Baby Home, and the alternative of confinement in a local hospital and a foster-mother for the baby – if one is available.

Mother and Baby Homes are in general becoming much more flexible about the length of time that their residents are expected to stay, but it is not usually less than one month before confinement and one month afterwards. This can look like an intolerably long absence to a girl who has never slept away from home in her life (and there are still a great many of these). It is understandable that some who are not prepared to face this exile, especially at a time of crisis, and others who are unwilling to look after their baby, beg the worker to find a foster-mother so that they can be confined in a hospital near their homes. (More will be said in the next chapter about the placing of babies for adoption straight from hospital, and the difficult question of how long a mother should care for her baby if she intends to offer him for adoption.) Indeed, the problem of finding the right solution for the individual pregnant girl is sometimes extraordinarily difficult, for the choice is always governed by what is available, and she sometimes projects her difficulties on to the outside world by steadfastly refusing, for no adequate external reason, a plan which would in fact be entirely workable if she would accept it. Immature and neurotic girls will often make desperate efforts to find a painless way out of their dilemma, and have the greatest difficulty in facing the inescapable fact that there is no solution which will spare them all suffering, and that all they can choose is what kind of suffering they will have: the risk of being recognised in the local hospital, or departure to another town; the anguish of parting with their baby or the pains and penalties of bringing him up themselves. The caseworker needs patience as well as skill and understanding to help her client to make a choice of painful remedies, and must strengthen her to stand by her decision once made.

Mother and Baby Homes have come in for a great deal of criticism in recent years. The need for more flexibility to enable them to meet new needs as they arise will be discussed later, but they remain an indispensable part of the available casework facilities. They can offer a fourfold helping service, quite apart from their usefulness as places to hide in from the scrutiny of friends and neighbours, which is often their first and only apparent advantage in the eyes of the girl and her parents. In the first place, there is the psychological benefit of being among others in the same position as the girl herself. It soon becomes clear to her that she is not the only person undergoing this ordeal, and she can see for herself that others come out safely on the other side of it. And it is a huge relief not to have to try to hold her stomach in and behave normally; no matter how big she gets there will always seem to be someone bigger than herself – and in worse situations too: girls with no homes, girls with physical, emotional or mental handicaps. A good Mother and Baby Home conveys a feeling of safety, of being protected not only from critical eyes but from Mother's nagging and perhaps from the attentions of the putative father. It provides a place in which she can think and talk about her baby's future and her own, without undue pressure from interested parties; and where, moreover, no one will be much surprised or upset if she has wild mood-swings or moments of hysteria. The quality of staff still varies greatly, but where they are good at their almost-superhuman task, life in the Home can be a revelation to its occupants, who quite often find a new mother-figure in the Superintendent or her Deputy.

Group therapy had been going on in Mother and Baby Homes for a long time before the name for it was found; the girls probably learn much more from the others in the group situation than from the staff.

The sense of fellowship, of all being in it together, operates in this small community, so that the individual members of it are influenced and disciplined by the group, and learn to tolerate and to share the good and the bad in each other. The shy girl is encouraged to take her due place, the aggressive one is quite efficiently flattened. The staff's role in the group is unobtrusive, and usually restricted to restraining any anti-social member who tends to become dominant. Naturally the group usually includes a fair cross-section of all the unmarried mothers in a fairly large catchment area, and there will be some who are seriously disturbed; but those few who fail to settle in and make a place for themselves are usually the ones who have been over-protected and spoilt. The great majority enjoy the experience of fellowship, and very often, after they return home, become wistfully reminiscent about the laughs they had over the washing-up or at someone's birthday party.

The third advantage that a Mother and Baby Home can offer is good physical care. Besides visits to the clinic, medical attention and relaxation classes, there will be plenty of good food, abundant hot water for baths and laundry, and ample time for rest and sleep – obvious benefits that by no means all pregnant girls can find in their own homes. It was primarily for this reason that the worker was so anxious that Dorothy (p. 27) should go away; ample diet and regular hours would have made a vast difference to her physical health, and her limited intelligence would have been stimulated in the fellowship of the household. Janet (p. 36) improved greatly in every way during her stay, although she deteriorated rapidly on returning home again. Brenda (p. 11), a shy and lonely girl, was more self-confident and had learnt to make herself more physically attractive by the time she left.

The fourth major service offered by the Mother and Baby Home is an opportunity to learn something of the arts of catering, cooking and housewifery, as well as knitting and sewing. A woman in her late twenties, happily married for some years, said: 'I never bring out my mixing-bowl without remembering Miss Ashley's "Get all your tools and ingredients together first." ' Help in preparing the baby's layette can guide the young mother in managing her money wisely, as well as showing her how to make practical and pretty clothes for her child.

Homes differ widely one from another, according to their history, location, size and staff. The specialist social worker knows well the ones in her area, and in discussing plans for confinement with her client she will be assessing which will be the most suitable. It is important for her to be clear as to whether the girl herself, and not only her mother, really wishes to go away from home, and why, but firm decisions are not usually made at the first interview unless the confinement is imminent. The client at this stage only needs information as to what the possibilities are, and what alternatives are open to her. These will be discussed in some detail, especially as regards clothing requirements, visiting times and finance.

For most pregnant girls, finance is not usually a major difficulty in the early stages. If they have been working steadily for the past eighteen months or so, they will qualify for National Insurance maternity benefit, and the fees at Mother and Baby Homes are geared to the current rate of the weekly allowance. The rest of the cost of the service to the girl is met by grants from the Local Authority to the Home under Part III, Section 22 of the National Health Service Act, 1943. In a certain small proportion of cases, the putative father will help financially; more will be said of this in a later chapter. Money problems are more likely to occur among the minority of girls who have not been working, perhaps because of some physical complaint such as asthma, or because they were needed at home. The Ministry of Social Security will usually help here, or in special circumstances the worker is able to approach various voluntary bodies such as the Buttle Trust, Thomas Coram's Foundation, Dr Barnardo's Homes or the Children's Society. Where schoolgirl mothers are concerned the Local Education Authority or the Children's Department will sometimes make a grant, or, failing this, most Mother and Baby Homes will make an assessment of what the parents can afford, and perhaps charge only a nominal sum in fees.

All these are practical matters which will usually have to be considered at the first interview, but while they are being discussed the interaction between worker and client continues to develop. The client should be able to perceive the worker's professional detachment and skill in her realistic approach to the problems, as well as her empathic acceptance of the client herself, and she will usually respond by becoming noticeably more relaxed and more co-operative. The worker will be arriving at a tentative diagnosis of the predisposing factors and precipitating circumstances of the pregnancy, and will have made some assessment of the strengths and weaknesses of the girl's personality. She will be aware, though, of the dangers of oversimplifying the situation or jumping to conclusions, and also of the difficulty of accurately separating the subjective from the objective in what her client has told her. For example, the girl may have said that her father was extremely kind and generous towards her, because she wanted to believe that this was so, and did not wish to acknowledge that she in fact found him cold and unapproachable.

Every caseworker tries to help her client to achieve deeper understanding of herself and her situation, so that she may manage better in future, and this is particularly so where illegitimacy is concerned; indeed it is the ultimate purpose of the whole casework process to release the unmarried mother from the adverse circumstances and the subjective drives which produced the situation, so that she may be enabled to live more fully and freely. This naturally is a long and delicate process, but it begins in the first interview when worker and client embark upon the casework relationship; one in which the client learns to trust the worker's unconditional acceptance of her as a person, and hence can begin to understand and accept herself. As the interview proceeds, the worker will begin to see some facets of the situation where a start can be made towards this goal. Valerie (p. 38) was encouraged to talk about her jealousy of her younger sister, and Fiona (p. 42) helped to face her bitter resentment of the fact that her mother had laughed scornfully when she said she was in love with Sandy. These, however, were not actually ventilated until a later stage in the casework process.

In the first interview, a start can be made to rebuild the client's self-confidence in small, practical ways which will help to convince her that she herself is in charge of the situation. She can fill in her own application form for maternity benefit (although Jane and Janet needed help with spelling), and can decide how to find her insurance number and when she will go to ask the doctor for her certificate of pregnancy. Success in even the smallest matters will bring valuable encouragement for the next, perhaps greater, effort.

Throughout this chapter it has been assumed that the interview takes place in the agency's office, as it usually does. This is convenient as saving the worker's time and affording the least risk of interruption, but home visits should always be made at a subsequent stage whenever it is possible and appropriate. The girl's greater self-confidence at home can help forward the casework relationship, and the worker can learn a great deal from seeing her against her own background. Valerie's home was eloquent of the life the family lived; Margaret threaded her way among spindly occasional tables set with immaculately kept ornaments; Janet's home was indescribably squalid. The home visit gives the worker a chance to assess the accuracy of the impressions she has received from what the girl has told her.

Ending the interview

The first interview will begin to draw to an end when the practical aspects of the situation have been discussed and some tentative plans made. There will be by this stage a great degree of crystallisation of the problem, and the pregnant girl frequently says: 'I feel so much better now that I've talked to you.' The wise caseworker will not actively encourage deeper confidences about her client's life history and sexual experience at this stage, although she will accept them if they are spontaneously offered; if the girl later feels that she has said too much to a complete stranger she may become more reserved in future, and it may be difficult to restore the free flow of the relationship. It is better to end on a practical note, with a clear understanding of what each has undertaken to do. The caseworker may have promised to get in touch with a colleague or make an enquiry about Social Security benefits, and her client may be committed to writing a letter to the putative father, visiting her doctor or telling her parents of the situation. Finally, a date will have been arranged for the next interview. By the time this comes round, the helping process will be well under way.

The experienced caseworker knows that it is a blunder to end on a note of false reassurance. A too-cheerful 'Don't worry, it'll come all right in time' is likely to draw some such reply as a bitter 'You don't have to go through with it'. In fact this facile optimism is the very negation of the empathic sharing in the situation that should be built up in the first interview. Rather, the client should leave with a conviction that here is someone who cares deeply, at her side and on her side.

It is usually best to write nothing down in the client's presence except names, addresses and other essential data, and the pregnant girl should never know that she will shortly have a case number and a file. But it is fervently to be hoped that after she has gone the worker will have five minutes in which to make some notes, as detailed as may be, and turn them face downwards on her desk before embarking on the next interview.

6. Coming to a Decision

Continuing casework

Before the second encounter both client and worker have time to assess what has already been done. The client perhaps feels a degree of reassurance at having met someone with experience in dealing with her situation, and who appears friendly and helpful. She may be prepared to respond, but this is not necessarily so. The worker's personality may not be congenial to her, or she may have had so little experience in forming relationships that she finds it difficult to do so. The girl with the greatest degree of emotional deprivation, and therefore the deepest need of love, will often be slow to react at first.

Many clients, however, will have been able to adjust their ideas about the situation as a result of information given to them at the first interview. The perceptive caseworker will be aware of the changes in her client's attitudes when they meet again.

She for her part will have thought carefully about her new client's problem, assessing the external situation, the character traits of the people concerned and the family dynamics. From what she has learned she will evolve a plan or policy which, although tentative and open to alteration as time passes, will nevertheless be clear and definite; she will not drift from one interview to the next with no objective in mind. At this stage she will almost certainly be aware of blank spaces in the picture she has gained, and will make a mental note that she needs to know more, for instance, about the pregnant girl's work, or her brothers and sisters. Discussion of these points at the second interview will continue the dialogue which builds up the relationship, and is likely to move on at the client's own pace, but with the worker's guidance, from practical matters to feelings and motives. Many clients are completely unused to expressing their emotions in words, and most will be shy and inhibited in talking about the circumstances of their baby's conception. The worker should be familiar with the expressions used locally for physical processes; these vary widely and would make a fascinating study in themselves. 'To be pregnant', for example, may be 'to be caught for', 'to be going to nurse', or 'to have fallen wrong'. The phrase 'to go with' a boy is widely used, but has many shades of meaning. The use of clear and simple language, which nevertheless avoids the extremes of local idiom, is one of the caseworker's skills. Some clients will need a further reassurance that what they tell the worker is strictly confidential before they talk of personal matters and deep feelings. The skilled caseworker will never give the impression that she is forcing confidences, but by means of tactful comments and her evident concern she will encourage the client to express what is in her mind.

As a result of this process the phenomenon known as 'transference' may arise. 'When we speak of transference reactions,' says Florence Hollis,[1] 'we usually mean that the client displaces on to the worker feelings or attitudes that he experienced in early childhood towards a member of his family – most often, but not necessarily, his father or mother – and responds to the worker as if he were this person.' This, of course, is no more than a specific instance of the way in which the pregnant girl's whole experience of life has made her what she is, but it is an observable fact that many girls whose relationship with their mothers was unsatisfying will see in the caseworker a new or substitute mother and will react accordingly. Hence the worker can give to her client an opportunity to work out her feelings, even, if necessary, by a marked regression towards childish dependence. Workers in Homes are especially familiar with this occurrence, and if they handle it well the girl may be enabled to grow through it. The caseworker will be aware of the possibility of a parallel reaction on her own part, known as counter-transference, and will be watchful lest her own associations from the past should distort her perception of present reality. Paul Halmos points out the need for scrupulous self-criticism to avoid indulgence, ambition and self-therapy in the involvement of the counsellor with the client, and he has a great deal to say about the medley of contradictions which the caseworker contrives to combine.[2] In the context of helping unmarried parents, the most conspicuous of these are:

The caseworker needs both 'spontaneous lovingness and scrupulously thought-out strategy of technique'; she must be intelligent, but her approach to the sexual relationship should not be coldly intellectual. She will be sensitive to the feelings of her clients, but never swayed by their emotion; she will feel with them in their guilt and anxiety, yet be clear-sightedly detached from it; she will offer them acceptance, but not ordinary friendship; she will not sit in judgment on their conduct, but neither will she condone wrongdoing; she will be identified with them in their predicament, but she will not project herself into it; she will offer her clients moral and emotional support, but will not tell them what to do; she will offer hope for the future, but not be falsely reassuring about the situation; and she will respect the privacy of her clients but enable them to be frank about their difficulties. More could no doubt be added to this list.

It is fortunate that the caseworker does not have to be consciously aware of her technique when confronting a nervous teen-ager. What matters then is the particular person before her, and how she may best be helped. During the second and subsequent interviews the interaction between client and worker continues to develop on two levels. From a practical point of view, and judging from appearances, they may be discussing a proposed application for Supplementary Benefit, but at the same time, by physical posture and facial expression, by glance of the eyes and tone of voice, another dialogue is in process. The pregnant girl may be conveying to the worker: 'I'm not altogether happy about this, because I dread going into that building and telling those officials that I'm pregnant, but because I want you to help me and therefore I don't want to offend you, I'm agreeing to go.' By the same means the worker may convey to her client: 'I perceive that you dislike this suggestion because you are shy by nature, especially in your present state, but I think you can do this and it will give you self-confidence if you deal with it successfully yourself.' This secondary dialogue is important, and quite often the worker will bring it into overt discussion, saying 'I don't think you like this suggestion, do you?' or 'I wonder how you feel about this?' in order to help her client to acknowledge her feelings. How much of the emotion attached to her condition, and especially to the circumstances of conception, the pregnant girl will be able to express, and how far she should be encouraged to do so, will depend mainly on her personality. It may be harmful for the psychotic girl to re-live her past experiences, but for the more normal ones it is often an inexpressible relief to talk freely about matters which have been too long bottled up inside them. A longish car journey is often an admirable opportunity for therapeutic conversation, and partly for this reason the worker should whenever possible take her client if she is to be admitted to a Mother and Baby

Home at a distance. This is an occasion on which supportive help is valuable. The client will appreciate not having to find her own way by public transport, and the worker in whom she has placed her confidence can help very much by her presence during this move to an unfamiliar life among strangers. 'I do wish it was me taking you,' sighed Brenda from the passenger seat, making a motion as though holding a steering-wheel.

While the girl is resident in a Mother and Baby Home there are two people responsible for her care: the Matron and the caseworker. Co-operation between them is essential, but sometimes proves difficult. The best foundation for it is, obviously, personal friendship and mutual understanding, and in any case the worker should realise the practical difficulties, for example, of letting the young mother come home for two nights without her baby in order to be interviewed for a job, while in her turn the Matron recognises the importance of the home background in plans made for the future. The administrative arrangements should be designed to promote smooth working. There should be a clear understanding as to how often the caseworker will visit her client, and who-does-what with regard to adoption arrangements or plans for the mother's return home with her baby. Each will keep the other informed of new developments, and case discussions between them can produce a clearer view of the situation which may be extremely valuable, as each sees the girl from her own particular standpoint. They should work closely together during the last weeks of her pregnancy and over the time of her confinement, particularly with regard to her future and that of her child.

The mother's responsibility

'On September 8th, to John and Jane Jones, a son.' The birth of a legitimate child is usually a matter for rejoicing, and even if he is 'one too many', so that his arrival creates grave difficulties of accommodation or finance, he nevertheless has an assured place in a family which is his by right, and two parents who are jointly concerned for his care. But the child born out of wedlock has no such security. There is no one whom he can call 'father'; his mother alone is legally responsible for him, and he cannot claim any sort of status but that of the bastard child. By some means or other he must be provided with, or at least as far as possible compensated for, what his birth has denied him: the safe background of a happy home and the love of two parents. How is this to be done?

In practice this very often comes down to a decision as to whether the mother should keep the child and bring him up herself, or offer him for adoption. This decision is crucial because it not only has a bearing on her own future and that of her immediate family, but will determine the whole lifetime of her child. One cardinal principle is thus apparent from the outset. The most important consideration is not what the mother is likely to feel if she takes one course rather than another, nor her own rights nor anyone else's over the child, nor what public opinion will say, but: What will be best for this particular child? This is the pivot on which the discussions should turn, and all the other questions that have to be asked are subsidiary.

As far as her capacities allow, the mother must herself face the problem and decide the question. There are two reasons why this should be so: in the first place the law invests in her alone the rights and duties of a parent, and secondly she has to live with the consequences for the rest of her life. Hence it is vitally important for her peace of mind that she should be satisfied that the resolution was for the real welfare both of her baby and of herself. It is fortunate that, as Jane Rowe points out,[3] the best interests of mother and child are in the long run one and the same; the wrong decision for the baby cannot be good for the mother, for at the end of the process she must be sincerely convinced that she 'did what was best' for the child if she is to come to terms with her own anxiety and guilt. Moreover she must not be allowed to feel that her decision was made without full knowledge of the alternatives open to her, that she made it hurriedly or on impulse, or that she was subjected to undue pressure.

This is the theory, or the ideal. It will at once be apparent that human contingency throws all sorts of difficulties in the way of its realisation. How is the fifteen-year-old to make a realistic decision about the upbringing of her baby? Her father will protest that she herself is a mere child, and that he is still legally responsible for her. Powerful emotions and biological drives enter into the situation too; the heart and the blood often override the brain. Social pressures and practical limitations may dictate the solution. Indeed, it may well be asked whether the mother actually has any real freedom at all. Some psychologists contend that her apparent decision is in fact almost predetermined by her mental and emotional make-up; they say that she may have a strong unconscious urge to present her baby to her dominating mother, or having 'got out of her system' her rage and spite against an authoritarian father she may lose interest in the baby and offer him for adoption without a qualm, as Leontine Young suggests. The sociologist might point to the strong pressures of conventional respectability in the mother's home background, or alternatively to the fact that illegitimate babies are easily accepted in her street. Moreover, many a mother who would dearly have liked to keep her baby is compelled by sheer economic necessity to part with him. Nevertheless the great majority of mothers show very real concern for the welfare of their baby, and the deep spring of their distress is the conflict between their rational awareness that the child would almost certainly be better off adopted and their own instinctual desire to mother him themselves. The fact that many undergo great uncertainty and stress of mind before coming to a decision shows that some – although necessarily limited – degree of choice is open to them.

Miss Yelloly says of her own study: 'the majority of the mothers made an apparently rational decision in which their primary consideration was concern for the wellbeing of their child. Most of them appeared to cope with the situation realistically and responsibly, and to grow through it. If we see such a girl's decision, whatever it may be, as an egotistic and irrational choice, we strip away her dignity, and remove the very elements in this sometimes bitter situation which have healing and constructive possibilities; for in the case of adoption, what makes this bearable at all for the mother is the conviction that she is acting in the best interests of her child, whatever the cost to herself. The possibilities of growth lie in the exercise of rational and responsible choice. There was no evidence that the adoption decision was determined by unconscious factors.'[4]

The caseworker's part

Jane Rowe says roundly that it is impossible for the worker to avoid the responsibility of playing a part in the decision about the child's future,[5] and indeed this is the focal point of all casework with unmarried parents. In this chapter it is assumed that the worker has been in touch with her client from an early stage in her pregnancy, so that she has had time to build up a warm supportive relationship with her.

Unfortunately this is not always so in practice, but it is extremely difficult to start casework help after confinement because, as will be seen presently, the beginnings of the long and complicated decision-making process usually come quite early in the pregnancy. This is a strong reason for early referral to a specialist worker.

The 'ifs and buts' of the principle of client self-determination are clearly seen in regard to the making of the decision about the future of an illegitimate baby. Obviously the worker does not encourage every mother to do just as she likes with her child; and even the independent or unco-operative client looks upon her caseworker as a person with knowledge and experience which she can bring to bear upon this particular situation. Whenever effective casework help is being given, the decision about the baby is bound to be the result of interaction between client and worker, which will involve a varying amount of direct influence. 'Self-determination is a relative, not an absolute, value. If the client is endangering others or himself, it must be superseded by another, the worker's responsibility to prevent suffering,'[6] says Florence Hollis.

In the first place, clients vary greatly in intelligence and in their natural capacity for resolution. Fr Beistek says: 'Caseworkers have differed in their evaluation of the capacity of unmarried mothers, as a group, to make sound decisions. Some feel that the unmarried mothers are so damaged emotionally that they are incapable of arriving at a good decision themselves. These caseworkers have expressed the conviction that they must guide, "steer" and "take sides" in the final decision. Other caseworkers seem to have a higher evaluation of the ability of unmarried mothers for self-determination. Both agree, however, that each unmarried mother's ability should be individually evaluated.'[7]

Secondly, it must be recognised that the pregnant girl is always under some degree of emotional strain; she may have given herself without reserve to a young man who has promptly forgotten her, leaving her bitterly frustrated and bewildered; or she may have been engaged and looking forward to her wedding day, but have suffered a revulsion, as a result of premarital intercourse and consequent feelings of guilt. In addition she has to cope with a major physical crisis, and the usual psychological stresses of pregnancy and childbirth are made worse by the fact that she has no husband to support her. She may indeed, on first seeing the worker, be so emotionally and physically exhausted as to be temporarily incapable of making even a minor decision for herself. In this case the worker will offer a protective relationship and play for time. A third factor is that there are always other people involved; the father of the baby, her parents, brothers and sisters and perhaps grandparents may all be affected by what she decides for her child, and all may have expressed their own views about what she should do. No wonder the client sometimes does not know where to begin. Perhaps the caseworker's greatest service to her client is to help her to keep the child's interests steadily before her eyes as the first consideration, so that she is not turned aside by her own emotions or the well-meant advice of friends and relatives. In particular she will be watchful that the child is never used as a means either to rehabilitate or to punish the mother, or to serve anyone else's purpose.

Within the framework of her steady acceptance of the client as a person in her own right, the caseworker must provide information as to the practical courses open to the mother, support her through the emotional difficulties and help her to think clearly and realistically about what will be best for her child and for herself. In all this she must maintain a most delicate balance between over-identification with the client in her dilemma, and too cold an objectivity. Two questions will often arise in the worker's mind: the first, 'If I'd become pregnant without having a wedding-ring, what would I have done with my baby?' and the second, 'If I'd had the bad luck to be born illegitimate, would I rather have grown up with my real mother but no father, or as an adopted child with two parents?' In the light of her answers to these questions, she will be the more on her guard against developing a bias in favour of either solution. It is all too easy, under the pressure of time and the demands of casework, to fall back upon stock answers, and to dogmatise to the effect that 'all children are better adopted' or that 'it's wrong to part a baby from its mother'. Until fairly recently it was the declared policy of many casework agencies, and of medical officers and public bodies also, to do everything possible to keep mother and child together. Research studies such as that carried out in Toronto[8] showed that this corporate prejudice resulted in great suffering and damage both to illegitimate children and to their mothers, and it has now practically disappeared under the influence of fuller and more exact psychological and sociological understanding. The dilemma of every unmarried mother is unique, and there is no ready-made answer to her problems.

A situation that has become much more common is that of the young couple, usually aged about eighteen, who are fully intending to marry when they can afford to do so, but who 'start a baby' prematurely. It may be impossible for them to marry immediately; the young man is earning apprentice's wages, and the girl will not be able to work if she keeps the baby. And where can they live together? There may be no room in their parents' houses, and lodgings are impossible to find, even if they could afford them. So what is to be done with the child? If he is adopted and his parents marry in due course, the eldest member of the family is missing – or they may never have another child. The alternative may be fostering for three years or more, and the dangers of this are obvious. And what guarantee is there that the young people will in fact marry one another? The worker has great practical and moral responsibilities in this predicament, and clear thinking is needed in assessing the situation.

The alternatives

The mother must know what alternatives are open to her, and it is the caseworker's duty not only to provide her with factual information about these, but to discuss them with her, objectively and at leisure, quite early in the helping process, before the emotional overtones of her decision make themselves too strongly felt. In the main there are four practical possibilities. She can keep the child with her and bring him up herself, living in her parents' home or in lodgings, or perhaps marrying a man who is not her baby's father; she can take a residential job where she can have the child with her, perhaps in the household of a doctor or where the wife has a full-time job of her own; she may place the child in a residential nursery; or she may offer him for adoption. None of these is ever the ideal solution, and all have obvious drawbacks, but it is also true that each of them has worked out well for some children and their mothers.

The difficulties that beset an illegitimate child growing up in his grandparents' home have been implied already. His mother is likely to be absent at work for the greater part of the day, and so it is Grandmother who looks after him. She may be elderly or ill, and moreover not necessarily at all willing to undertake the task in the first instance. 'I just don't feel like fighting with another, but I suppose I shall have to – poor little thing!' sighed a Granny whose daughter had insisted on keeping her baby. Or it may be Grandfather who is unwilling to put up with nappies round the fire and disturbed nights. Dissension is almost bound to come, perhaps when the mother, who has been at work all day while Grandmother was coping with a fretful baby, 'gets dressed' after tea and goes off to the pictures. Equally often, mother and grandmother disagree about the handling of the child; mutual accusations of spoiling or harshness are made, and tempers rise. Arguments in the child's presence corrode his security, and make it perfectly plain to him that he is not wanted. He may react with timidity and self-effacement, or by aggression, but in either case his suffering is great, and it will be difficult for him to grow up into a healthy well-adjusted person. Even in a united family where there is tolerance and generosity, he is seldom sure of his status. It is as important for an illegitimate child to know his real mother as it is for an adopted child to know that he is adopted, and with wise adult help to understand his true position, but this does not often happen. It is so much less trouble in the early stages to let him call his grandmother 'mother' and to think of his real mother, whom he knows by her Christian name, as a big sister, but the difficulties begin on the day when one of his schoolmates shouts 'You've got no father', and uses the dread word 'bastard'. Then his insecurity is made much worse by the knowledge that the grown-ups whom he trusted have lied to him about a matter so important as his own origin.

Many social workers have found that domestic crises of one kind or another occur frequently in the lives of illegitimate children. If his mother disappears or loses interest, he may be handed from grandmother to aunt, taken into care for a time, fostered out, returned to relatives and, as it seems to the child, generally pushed around until he becomes a typical delinquent disturbed child. The stories of Dorothy (p. 27) and Jane (p. 11) show clearly how illegitimacy can be self-perpetuating in circumstances like these. It is true that Dorothy was exactly one-third of Jane's age, and rather more intelligent, but both had been born illegitimate, and both their mothers had subsequently left home. Jane's teen-age behaviour had been very similar to Dorothy's; she had apparently become 'man-mad' and spent her time looking for pick-ups in a desperate search for the close relationships she had never had.

Even if the illegitimate child continues in his mother's care, her marriage is likely to bring further hazards, for in spite of their protestations and sincere good intentions beforehand, there are not many husbands who can accept another man's child so completely that his presence neither arouses discord nor aggravates it, and the illegitimate child will be very sensitive to the subtlest distinctions made between himself and the children of the marriage. However, it is also true that in the life histories of many illegitimate children these difficulties have either not arisen or have been surmounted. A certain number are adopted by the mother and her husband, and where this arrangement is successful it is probably the happiest of all solutions to the problem of illegitimacy, for the child both keeps his own mother and loses the stigma of his birth status. But everything depends on the attitude of the adoptive father and the adjustment of the mother to the situation, and there are many hazards.

The difficulties of life with an illegitimate child in rooms or lodgings have already been referred to, and are well known. Success depends on too many variables: the goodwill of the landlady, a day nursery or a satisfactory 'minder' for the baby, steady work bringing in an adequate income, and the good health of both mother and child. Yet some mothers have found it preferable to the tyranny of ageing parents, and a few who had no other home have made a happy life for themselves, as Miss M. did (p. 32).

The mother who takes a residential job with her baby needs a capacity for organisation as well as adaptability and determination. It is often difficult to reconcile the claims of her work and the child; baby may have to be left to cry while the doctor's dinner is served or the telephone answered. Also the amount of money she receives is usually small because her own keep and that of the baby are taken into account as part of her pay. Saving is therefore difficult, and also off-duty time without the baby may be a problem. Moreover, if the mother loses her job or finds it unsuitable she gives up her home as well when she leaves, and this can be harmful for her child. Nevertheless, such posts have proved to be happy solutions for some girls, and in particular they have the great advantage of allowing the mother to look after her baby herself. One professional woman has had four unmarried mothers to help in the house, all of whom have left to be married. Another girl has in effect become a member of her employer's family, and her son is doing well at Grammar School.

The work of John Bowlby has made it so abundantly clear that institutional upbringing is a very poor second best for any child that social workers avoid it whenever possible. Even so, great efforts are being made to remove its disadvantages, and for a few babies it is the best, or the only possible, solution. For instance, the child of a very inadequate girl who had no home of her own proved to be severely handicapped with spina bifida. On discharge from hospital he was received into care by the Children's Department and well looked after in their nursery. All three of Jane's previous children (p. 11) had been accepted into the care of voluntary organisations, and two were later placed by them for adoption. For the baby of partly African or West Indian blood, too, nursery upbringing is often the only plan, since there are far too few adopters who feel able to accept a coloured child. Many voluntary bodies have been obliged to restrict the number of such babies in their homes, but in the long run it may be an advantage for children who unfortunately start with a handicap in present-day society to grow up in fellowship with one another, and in the care of people who by experience have become expert in handling their particular difficulties.

Two other possible alternatives should perhaps be mentioned: marriage to the child's father, and placing him with foster-parents. Forced weddings are so seldom really successful that they can be ruled out as a means of providing a happy and secure home for a child. The only valid reasons why two people should marry are, first, that they desire a lifelong relation with one another, and secondly that this relationship seems good in itself from all points of view. Hence it follows that to marry for the sake of giving a child a home, or a name, is an extravagant misuse of a great human potentiality. The child automatically becomes the focal point for any strain in the marriage, and in measure as his security is impaired the original (mistaken) purpose of the marriage is defeated. And few situations are more bitter than that of a young couple who have 'had to get married', as they thought, but whose child has not survived, leaving them unwillingly linked together for no apparent purpose.

Fostering is sometimes seized upon by the more unrealistic and unstable mother as the right solution for her because it offers a compromise: the baby remains hers, but she does not have to look after it. In fact, and for this same reason, it is the least satisfactory of all the possible ways of dealing with the problem. A clear distinction should here be made between short-term fostering until the baby is placed for adoption at the age of six or eight weeks, which will be considered more fully in the chapter on adoption, and the much vaguer arrangement, with no clear-cut time limit, which usually starts with an understanding that the mother will have her baby back 'when she gets a job' or 'when she's got somewhere to live'. Weeks and months may pass with a succession of excuses and delays, while payments for the child's keep may fall into arrears and the mother perhaps disappears altogether, leaving the foster-parents with a growing toddler to whom they may become deeply attached, and complete uncertainty as to his future. This problem has already been referred to in Chapter 2. The social worker will do her best to prevent this situation from developing, for her own experience bears out John Bowlby's contention that continuity of care from the earliest days is essential for the child's wellbeing, and that therefore he should be settled in his permanent home by the time he is two or three months old, with the absolute minimum of changes before that age. This creates especial difficulties for the type of girl who, being emotionally unable to commit herself to a decision, may take several months to come to the point where she can admit that her hope of being able to have the baby with her is a fantasy with no realistic foundation. The caseworker must use all her skill and understanding to help the girl to face the facts in the interests of her baby and bring her to the point of decision. The limitations on a client's freedom for self-determination apply quite specifically to the decision about her baby: she must not do what is bad for him. English law is grossly inconsistent in this respect. The Guardianship of Infants Act, 1935, requires that the child's wellbeing must be the primary consideration in all arrangements made for him, but in practice we cling to the old concept of parental rights even where these are obviously in conflict with the child's good, so that it would be illegal to make arrangements for his adoption without the mother's consent, whatever the circumstances. Section 3 of the Adoption Act, 1950, which empowers the Court to dispense with consent if it is 'unreasonably withheld', has never been interpreted to cover an arrangement made without the mother's consent in the first place. A judgment made by Mr Justice Pennycuick in 1962 did, however, establish that a parent's refusal to consent could be overruled if he had failed in his 'natural and moral duty to show affection, care and interest towards his child'.[9] It is time the concept of 'possession' of a child was removed from our thinking, and from the law.

James's father was a Pakistani, and because of his colour it proved impossible to find adopters for him. His mother's family, although they were unable to make a home for him themselves, were distressed at the prospect of his being brought up in an institution, and when an apparently suitable family suggested having him as a foster-child, their offer was gratefully accepted. When James was just two years old his father, who had been contributing regularly to the child's maintenance, said that he wanted to adopt him. Thereupon a complicated situation rapidly developed; his foster-parents asserted that they had been on the point of announcing their own wish to adopt James, and his mother, piqued by the marriage of James's father to someone else, declared that she would never consent to his adoption by his father but would be willing to let the foster-parents have him. In the meantime, grave doubts about their suitability had arisen, on grounds of physical health and also of their attitude towards James since adoption was first mentioned. A long period of uncertainty and tension resulted, which had a bad effect on James himself. The worker had acted in good faith in first placing the child, but made a mistake in not formulating a clear-cut policy as to the child's future.

Leontine Young, however, gives instances of long-term fostering leading on successfully to adoption.[10] In Great Britain, long-term fostering 'with a view to adoption' is widely practised, especially where there are queries about the physical health or mental endowment of the child. This is often satisfactory in the circumstances, but its success depends largely on the fullest possible medical, psychological and social information about mother, child and foster-home before placement, and clear planning and skilled handling throughout.

In all the schemes outlined above the natural mother retains legal and financial responsibility for her baby. None, however, guarantees the presence of a father-figure in the child's life, but adoption does this as far as can be foreseen. From the child's point of view there is no doubt that, in general, adoption offers much the best prospect of a happy and permanent home with the love of two parents, but it demands of the mother the ability to surrender her child completely. This is nearly always painful. Hence it is easy to see why social workers have found that, apart from a few who are pathologically indifferent, it is nearly always the most intelligent and the psychologically well-balanced mothers who are able to offer their babies for adoption. And even this course is not a perfect solution, because the happiest adopted child must at some point, probably in his teens when he is at his most sensitive, come face to face with the fact that he was born illegitimate.

These, then, are the possible solutions open to the unmarried mother in deciding the future of her child. Naturally, no pregnant girl will consider them all equally dispassionately; some will have made up their minds before they ever see the social worker, and others will in hard fact have no choice at all. If Grandfather refuses to allow the child to go home and the mother has not the qualities she would need to live independently, either in a residential job or in lodgings, she must be helped to accept adoption in her child's interests, in spite of her own reluctance. It may comfort her greatly if she has discussed the situation fully with a sympathetic caseworker.

Together, the caseworker and her client will come down to brass tacks about the situation in front of them. They will assess the financial prospects: how much can the mother expect to earn? Will she be entitled to any statutory benefits, and what are the prospects of financial help from the putative father? In particular, what evidence has she for obtaining an affiliation order? Then there are the practical details as to where she will live, and who will help her to look after the child. In all these discussions it is the caseworker's duty – and not always an easy one – to help her client to be firmly realistic and factual. But mixed up with the externals are the 'imponderables' which are even more important, and it is here that the caseworker has knowledge and skill which the mother cannot normally be expected to have. Is the client's blithe confidence that 'Dad will come round to the idea' of her keeping the baby justified, or not? And what will be the consequences if she is mistaken? The worker, applying her knowledge of family dynamics to the situation before her, may come to the conclusion that the grandfather could very well use the child as a tool to provoke strife between mother and grandmother, on account of an underlying hostility towards his wife. In her objective assessment of the situation this possibility is likely to outweigh the fact that there does not seem to be any material difficulty, since the mother's earning capacity is good and there is room in the house for the baby.

The worker does not, however, immediately and directly attempt to share this insight with her client. If the mother were to be told in so many words that her father might 'turn against' her for taking the baby home, the likely result could be a violent reaction of indignation and possibly an accusation against the worker of meddling with the family's life. Nevertheless her knowledge of the situation will influence the worker's approach; she may encourage her client to reflect upon her relations with her father in the past, so that she may come to see the same truth for herself and accept it realistically.

The grounds for the choice

Naturally, the mother's emotions play a very great part in the choice, and her decision will be closely linked with the predisposing factors in the pregnancy. The girl who shows a strong maternal instinct from the start, and long before the child is born insists that she could not bear to part with him because she will love him too much, will keep the child because she wanted a baby. This is a common reaction in immature girls from unhappy homes; the baby is their 'very own'. The prospects for the child are poor, because the mother is likely at first to be intensely possessive and demanding, and then when she finds that the child cannot give her the security she needs she is likely to reject him. Such mothers often find it difficult to realise that the child will be an individual person, with a mind and will of his own, and that moreover he will not be a helpless infant for long but will grow into a demanding youngster. The worker can help by keeping her client in touch with the realities of the situation, but it will be difficult to get her to accept any insight into her own motives, and she may refuse even to consider adoption. This kind of mother often needs long-term casework help as she brings up her child, but unfortunately she seems especially liable to become antagonistic to the worker and sever the connection. If this happens a referral to a new worker in the Children's Department as a preventive case may be useful.

Quite often the girl who has been dominated by her father feels vindictive against men in general, and uses her baby as a weapon. Every caseworker is familiar with the unmarried mother who vows she will 'make the man pay' for what has happened, and gets sadistic satisfaction out of the Court proceedings for an affiliation order. Other girls who have been dominated are so submissive that they part with their babies and resume daily life without a protest. Sometimes, if the client has not been weakened too much, the worker may be able to help her to build up some degree of independence for herself. Many pregnant girls feel an indifference towards the baby about to be born, and some cultivate this feeling in the hope that it will lessen the pangs when he is placed for adoption, but it is part of the caseworker's task to prepare such a girl for the possibility of a strong upsurge of maternal feeling once the child has arrived, or as soon as labour begins. The worker must understandingly support the mother in skilful handling of this strong emotion, perhaps by helping her to see that there are many kinds of love. Some are so possessive as hardly to deserve the name at all. 'I'm keeping him, he's mine,' says the girl who has been emotionally starved. A more realistic love may lead a girl to look at all the difficulties of unmarried motherhood fairly and squarely, and decide that she and her child will face them together, come what may. But it is possible that the most unselfish kind of all will choose the strongest chance of security and happiness for the child, and decide in faith upon adoption in spite of the mother's own grief and loss in consequence. The caseworker must be able to assess what kind and degree of love her client is capable of.

Where the mother has some scope for effective choice about the future of her baby, in that it appears to be physically and economically possible for her to keep the child if she decides to do so, she should be helped to look at her own motives for the decision. 'If I keep him, everybody will know' sometimes seems a powerful reason for adoption, but a more perceptive client can be helped to go on to reflect that even if she parts with him it will not make any difference to the fact that she had an illegitimate child, and that she will have to decide with every subsequent boy-friend whether he is 'serious' enough to have to be told. Is Mavis keeping her baby as an expiation for the hurt to her father, or as a punishment for herself, or as a threat to the young man who jilted her? Are her parents taking up one of these attitudes? None is in the least conducive to the child's welfare.

Margaret Yelloly concludes from her research that 'unstable or emotionally disturbed mothers are more likely to keep their children, despite the presence of characteristics which would ordinarily tend towards adoption'. John Bowlby, by contrast, comments on a study made in New York: 'Only if at least four of the following conditions are present is the mother likely to take the baby home: that she is a stable personality, takes a sensible attitude towards her problem, is loving and accepting of the child, really cared for the supposed father, and has a family which does not insist on the child being disposed of.'[11] In fact, every specialist worker knows that both these apparently contradictory views are right in some cases. There are intelligent, emotionally balanced young women like Alison (p. 41) who decide that adoption is in the best interests of their baby, and there are others, equally mature, who undertake to bring up their child themselves. Miss M. (p. 32) was one of these. On the other hand there are many girls like Janet (p. 36) and Dorothy (p. 27), the immature and unstable ones who cling to their babies, whom Miss Yelloly had in mind. Also there are a few emotionally disturbed girls who can let their child go with no sign of feeling.

It is very clear that for a great many unmarried mothers the scope for rational decision, although it does exist, is severely limited by practical and psychological considerations. Indeed, certain American psychiatrists are now claiming that they can correctly predict the outcome of the decision in 80 per cent of cases. The specialist caseworker has a duty to acquire and test out the new knowledge which is being gained from research, in order to improve her own service to her clients. The deeper her theoretical understanding the better, because at bottom her part in the process of deciding the child's future is to provide, with a warm heart, the informed, far-sighted, constructive, rational hard-headedness that the mother, in the nature of things, cannot usually be expected to have.

The timing of the decision

In the last chapter it was pointed out that arrangements for the confinement cannot be made without at least a tentative idea of what is planned for the child's future. If the mother has quite decided to bring him up herself and there seem to be no obstacles to this, there is not usually much point in her going away to a Mother and Baby Home although she may choose to do so; but if there is even a slight element of doubt she will not wish to have the child in her own familiar surroundings, unless and until she has made up her mind to keep him. Hence it is apparent that the baby's future is a live issue from a very early stage in the pregnancy. At what point is a firm decision made?

In general, it would seem that the more mature, intelligent and healthy mothers go through a period of extreme distress and anxiety in the first two months of their pregnancy, but then, as they start to adjust to the situation, the future of the baby becomes one of their main concerns. Hence casework help, which at the very beginning is simply supportive in character, is then directed to helping the mother to make a wise decision. It is impossible to be explicit about the time when the baby's future is finally settled, for there is very seldom any clear-cut moment of decision; the mother's thoughts and feelings turn in one direction or another, she tries out the situation in her mind and may change her inclination two or three times before deciding on her course of action. And even after her decision is made she is likely to waver in some degree.

All the same it is abundantly clear that the great majority of mothers who receive casework help have more or less made up their minds about the child's future before the birth takes place, and quite a number know what they will do from an early stage in the pregnancy. Of one hundred pregnant girls chosen at random from the agency in which the material for this book was gathered, forty-nine kept their babies and fifty-one offered them for adoption. Thirty-six had decided, as far as can be seen, before the sixth month of their pregnancy began – nine that they would keep their babies, and twenty-seven for adoption. Between the sixth month and the birth of the child, it seems that another forty-seven mothers had made their decision: twenty to keep their babies, and twenty-seven for adoption. Thus 83 per cent of mothers had decided before their baby was born. Of the seventeen who did not make up their minds until after the child's birth, fifteen kept their babies and two offered them for adoption. These figures are approximate because the records are incomplete, but they compare interestingly with Margaret Yelloly's study[12] which showed that about 67 per cent of mothers had made up their minds before the child's birth.

This touches upon one of the most controversial points in casework with unmarried mothers. The Adoption Act of 1950 says that no mother may give her consent to adoption until the child is six weeks old, and until fairly recently it was almost universally assumed that it was both unrealistic and unfair to expect a girl to make a decision about the future of her baby until she had recovered from the physical and emotional effects of her pregnancy and confinement. It was felt that the ongoing process was quite enough for her to cope with, and that she should not have the additional ordeal of facing a future parting with her baby – which is what it amounts to for about 25 per cent of all unmarried mothers, and a much higher proportion of those who come for casework help, as we have seen. This may be sound psychological sense, as well as humane; the mind prefers to cope with one predicament at a time. But perhaps it was not fully realised that the decision about the baby is an essential part of the pre-natal anxiety, and that this anxiety may be reduced by the knowledge that the child's future is more or less settled. Every experienced caseworker has met many girls who are eager to make firm plans for adoption before the baby is born, and they naturally counter this with a suggestion that it will be best to have the baby in the cot first. It is possible also that workers have been misled by dramatic changes of plan after the baby is born; the proportion of cases in which this happens is in fact very small, but they command attention by the amount of work and emotional adjustment they require. New psychiatric and sociological knowledge is making it easier to forecast these sudden reversals. Perhaps the most realistic approach to the mother's decision is to regard it as having two distinct phases: a tentative conclusion before the baby is born, and a final ratification afterwards. This allows for the flexibility which is vitally necessary in all the plans made at this stage, while at the same time recognising that the mother has decided to some extent.

To quote Miss Yelloly: 'This a topic fraught with difficulty. From the fierce dissension which it arouses in any discussion, it is clear that for many of us strong identifications, with mother or with child, tend to cloud our judgment. It is difficult to distinguish well-founded arguments from the rationalisations which protect us from the need to change; to sift evidence from opinion. In perhaps no other area of social work is compassion so confused with envy, the desire to serve mixed with the wish to punish.'[14]

Between the decision and the parting

It would help to reduce the temperature of debate on this subject if a clear distinction were made between two steps which are quite separate but are nearly always confused in discussion: the making of the decision for adoption, and the actual parting of mother and child. How long should elapse between the two is a matter of the greatest importance, and it is most desirable that a clear-cut but flexible plan should be agreed upon between the client and her worker before the baby is born. This plan will take account of all the circumstances, from the mother's psychological state and her own wishes to the availability of a foster home. Thirty years ago many voluntary organisations had a rule that mother and child should stay together for a full three months after the baby's birth. The reasons for this were never very clear, but there was certainly a punitive element: the girl who had offended against society by having an illegitimate baby must not be allowed to shuffle off her responsibilities lightly, and if the parting ultimately caused her suffering that was no more than just. Later the period was reduced to six weeks, and the desire to punish the girl is now less evident, but many experienced workers are convinced that the majority of unmarried mothers need a month or two in which to prepare themselves for the parting with the baby. Certainly they should never be hurried, and a considerable number of girls are like Deborah who said: 'All the time I was in labour I wanted nothing but to have my baby in my arms and hold him close. I couldn't have borne to part with him right away, but now that I've mothered him for a bit and seen him come on, I can hand him over to his adopters feeling that I know him as a person.' Deborah was balanced and mature, but it may be equally helpful for the very young mother, and the psychopathic girl who is unable to form a real relationship with anyone, to look after the baby for long enough to realise that he is not just a doll to be pushed about in a pram, or a weapon to use against someone else, but a real person whose care demands a routine of hard work. These mothers can then offer their babies for adoption more willingly than if they were left to cherish unreal fantasies about them.

Rose Bernstein, in a most stimulating contribution to the symposium entitled *The Unwed Mother*,[15] says: 'In general, it might be well to examine our uncritical assumption that for the mother who must relinquish her child early separation is invariably indicated. Perhaps we need to consider the possibility that there are differences in the rates at which biological ties between mothers and babies are loosened, just as there are differences in the strength of these ties; that variations in the timing of the separation may therefore be indicated; that a premature separation may be as injurious as indefinite temporising; and that perhaps the community has a responsibility to furnish the resources whereby such individual differences can be provided for.'

On the other hand there are girls who are so afraid to love their babies, knowing that they cannot keep them, that they literally hold them at arm's length. There are others who reject the child completely because of the circumstances of his conception or the associations with his father, or project on to the baby their own guilt and anger. The effect these mothers have on their babies cannot be good, and experience shows that they do not thrive. An early parting is certainly best in these circumstances. Caseworkers now find, moreover, that there are increasing numbers of intelligent girls who are fully aware that many psychiatrists advocate the placing of the baby in his adoptive home as early as possible, and this knowledge reinforces their own wish to get the ordeal over and return quickly to normal life. Such girls provide a crucial test of the caseworker's adjustment to the situation. Why does she hang back? Is it because she retains a trace of the wish to punish, and feels that the girl is being let off too lightly? Or is she afraid that the young mother will change her mind and recall her baby? Or that it will seem unfair to the other girls in the Mother and Baby Home who are staying for six weeks? Or is she just unwilling to accept fresh thinking on this problem of when is the best time to part? She needs to be most watchfully honest about her own approach, and must search always for the real wellbeing of the individual baby and his mother.

Unfortunately it still sometimes happens that mothers who are able and willing to look after their babies pending adoption are subjected to pressure to breast-feed them. A few, though not many, such mothers will sincerely wish to suckle their babies; but it seems an unnecessary cruelty thus to strengthen the emotional bond with her child in the unwilling mother who is least able to cope with its severance. 'Rigid policies that all unmarried mothers must care for their babies for three or six months and must breast-feed them can have no place in a service designed to help illegitimate babies and their unmarried mothers to live happy and useful lives,' says John Bowlby.[16] Rose Bernstein, however, suggests another point of view: 'For most unmarried mothers this is a first experience in motherhood and as such it may be an important influence in the image a girl establishes of herself as a mother-person. Part of our goal should be to help her to emerge from it with as positive an image of herself as a mother as her personality and circumstances will permit. To do this we need to be ready, at appropriate times, to de-emphasise the unmarried, socially deviant aspect of her experience and accentuate its normal motherhood components. In fact we may well ask ourselves whether, in failing to exploit the full possibilities of motherhood for the unmarried mother, we may not be encouraging the blocking out of large areas of affect in her experience in maternity, whether she is surrendering her baby or keeping it.'[17] Alison (p. 41) certainly was very conscious that she might never have another baby, and entered fully into the whole process of her pregnancy and childbirth. The experience of motherhood in itself should certainly be made as satisfying as it can be for the unmarried girl; workers in residential homes and hospital staff are sometimes highly skilled in this.

In any case, whether the separation comes early or late, it is nearly always anguish; there is no painless solution. As in the decision between adoption and keeping the baby, the mother can only choose which kind of pain she will have. But the worker can do a great deal to help her client to take a positive view of the adoption decision by her own attitude and the language she uses, if for example she speaks of 'offering the baby for' adoption or 'giving him to' adopters rather than of giving the child up or letting him go, and it is a real help to many girls to know that their baby brings joy to a childless couple. Again, many have peace of mind if they sincerely feel that they did everything they could for their baby while he was in their care, and that he passed from one loving home to another.

Many pregnant girls assert at some stage that they do not wish even to see their baby, usually because they are afraid to love the child. It is best not to accept this as a final decision. Even if the mother is not going to handle her child at all she will nearly always wish to see him once he is born, and it almost invariably proves to be much better for her peace of mind that she should do so. 'I might as well have drowned him like a kitten,' said one mother after ten years of bitter regret at having so completely rejected her child. A notable exception was Violet, who had had meningitis in infancy. A child herself, she adored all babies; the gynaecologist insisted that she must not see her child, and Violet accepted this as being 'best for her and Baby'. Here is an instance in which the client's capacity for self-determination was very limited indeed.

Judy was an intelligent girl of middle-class background who became pregnant as a result of her friendship with an Italian. He was too poor to marry her, and they separated. Shortly afterwards, when Judy was no more than four months pregnant, she met and very quickly married Robert, a Scotsman whose family background was similar to her own. It was obvious, however, that the expected baby could not be his child. Judy herself, who was profoundly in love with Robert, felt that she must offer her baby for his sake, even though

Robert himself was willing to accept the child and asked many searching questions as to how he would be brought up by adoptive parents. She insisted, however, that she could not and would not handle her baby, although she saw him soon after he was born. She needed little help in making and carrying out her plan, and in this was very unlike Miss M. (p. 32), whose daughter was almost six weeks old before she finally made up her mind against adoption after many long discussions with her caseworker.

Freda was a girl who in the course of casework changed her mind completely. When she first came to the agency she wanted to go to a Mother and Baby Home for the last month of her pregnancy and return straight home on discharge from hospital, and the baby was to be fostered pending adoption. She was so adamant about this that she succeeded in persuading the Matron of the Mother and Baby Home to agree. As time passed her attitude changed; the fostering, she now said, was to be so that she could make quite certain about adoption. When the baby was born, however, all her hesitations were resolved and she took her baby home with her. She had needed time and opportunity to work through her doubts and misgivings.

Once the decision to offer the baby for adoption is made, the caseworker must support the mother in carrying it out. She will be sensitively aware of her client's feelings about parting with her baby, which may vary from indifference to deep distress, but her own attitude will have a profound influence upon the mother. Many clients feel relief at having arrived at a firm plan which they feel will be in the child's best interests, and being thus enabled to come to terms with their grief and guilt, will execute it without further misgivings; others may falter, being less sure of the rightness of their decision or of their ability to go through with a parting. The caseworker will need sympathy and firmness to reassure a client who may try her patience considerably. Sometimes it is necessary for a worker to act with strength to uphold a commitment to adoption, where this is quite obviously in the best interests of the child.

Anne was a spoilt and unstable girl whose Beatnik boy-friend was completely unacceptable to her widowed mother. When she became pregnant she insisted that her baby be placed from hospital with foster-parents pending adoption, saying that she 'never intended the brat and didn't want it', but soon after this plan was put into effect, in a characteristic mood-swing she changed her mind, announcing that she and Ray were going to make a home together and that her mother would look after the baby for three months or so until they were ready for him. Baby Mark was moved to Grandmother's care, but as time passed it became apparent that his parents were making no attempt to provide for him; the father was sent to prison for a motoring offence and Anne neither visited the child nor paid anything for his maintenance, while Grandmother became exhausted in looking after him. Anne's caseworker succeeding in persuading her to consent to Mark's being placed for adoption, and at the same time Anne freely promised that she would not change her mind. A month later she wrote to say that she wanted Baby back in a few weeks' time; the caseworker decided to ignore her letter, and there were no further developments for nearly two months, except that Anne changed her job, left her lodgings and could not be found. Then she again made an attempt to reclaim Mark. After a long and difficult interview she agreed to sign her legal consent to his adoption, but there were more delays and procrastinations, and it was over a year before the order was made. Mark in the meantime had settled happily with most suitable adopters, and it obviously would not have been in his interests to accede to his mother's requests for his return.

To sum up, the first consideration in deciding the future of the illegitimate child must always be his real welfare. The worker participates in the decision by offering information, by helping the client to think realistically, and by supporting her throughout the operation.

The decision, then, has been made and the moment of parting which begins the adoption process is approaching. The preparations for this, and the mother's giving of her baby, are discussed in the next chapter.

7. Adoption: Casework with the Mother

When should a baby be adopted?

There are some guide lines which are helpful in coming to a decision, although it is true that every child is unique and his individual circumstances must be carefully evaluated.

It has already been stressed that the child's welfare is of paramount importance, and must always take first place. He must never be used to someone else's purpose, and it is in avoiding this that the caseworker's greatest difficulty may arise. For example, grandparents sometimes take up a punishing attitude towards their daughter, and propose to keep the baby 'so that she'll have to stay in at nights to look after it', or even as a sort of restitution for their own assumed failure in bringing her up; or alternatively they insist that she must part with the child. The worker has the responsibility of seeing that the baby's welfare is not lost sight of in the jungle of family interactions.

Also, the worker may be made profoundly unhappy at times because she finds herself unable to prevent what she feels sure is a wrong decision. From all objective points of view it would appear to be disastrous that Dorothy (p. 27) insisted on keeping her baby; she was herself much too immature and emotionally stunted to mother the child effectively, and moreover it was her grandmother, a sick and incapable woman herself, who took care of the baby. Dorothy's earnings were very small, and she had no evidence for an affiliation order. Hence the baby was environmentally handicapped from the start, and the caseworker had to contend with Dorothy's unwillingness to cooperate in ensuring the child's real wellbeing. But in law the mother carries the sole responsibility for the illegitimate child. The worker can only remind herself that after all she is not omniscient, and that the outcome may prove to be much better than might be expected. All she can do is to alert the Health Visitor and perhaps the Children's Department, as was suggested in the last chapter.

The primary and basic need of every child is for security. This has two aspects; the first and most essential is the emotional one, in that he must have a permanent, unconditional relationship of love with someone who mothers him (although this need not necessarily be his natural mother) and with a father and other family figures; the second is for a daily life and a dwelling-place which ensure him reasonable continuity of experience; hence housing conditions and finance are important. If the mother cannot provide this security in one or other respect, then adoption is strongly indicated.

It is not every unmarried mother who wants to keep her baby. A certain number of girls are psychopathically unable to form a maternal relationship, and others may reject their child because the circumstances of his conception arouse in them strong anger, guilt or shame. It would be a great mistake to try to persuade these mothers to bring up their babies themselves. Other girls may at first resolve to keep their baby for totally wrong reasons, such as vindictiveness towards the father or in the mistaken hope that the growing child will be able to offer them the love they are still looking for. By means of such insight into their own motives as they are capable of, and by constant stress on the welfare of the child, they should be helped to accept adoption.

The maturity and capability of the mother is the most important element in the situation, and, as Margaret Yelloly says, 'It is difficult to apply any general hypothesis in relation to an adoption decision without an accurate diagnosis of the mental and psychological condition of the mother.'[1] It takes character to bring up an illegitimate child successfully. Attention should, however, also be given to her family relationships and domestic circumstances. Will the baby be genuinely welcome at home? Who will look after him while his mother is at work? Are her lodgings likely to be really satisfactory? Will she be able to support her child? Any doubts on this score are strong pointers towards adoption as the wiser solution. The attitude of the putative father is relevant; he may be able and anxious to help the mother and child, even if marriage is not intended. Or on the contrary he may deny all responsibility, and in this case, if she has no proof of paternity, the mother may be influenced towards adoption. Again, what are her feelings towards her child's father? Sometimes, if he is married, the mother will resolve upon adoption out of loyalty to him; whether he is or not she may cherish a hope, however unrealistic, that they may ultimately marry, and hence be inclined to keep her baby. If she feels vindictive towards him, she is likely to do the exact opposite of whatever he has said.

Miss Yelloly lists eight factors, three of which tend especially strongly towards a decision in favour of adoption: the presence at home of other children of the natural mother, the fact that the putative father is a married man, and a negative attitude on the part of the maternal grandparents. The other factors which she found to encourage the decision in favour of adoption were: social class, adoption being more frequent among professional groups and those who had been educated at grammar or private schools; strained family relationships in general, or a broken family unit; the fact that the mother was under eighteen years of age; and the fact that the mother was not living at home when the child was conceived. None of these factors is decisive in itself, however, and their individual relevance will vary according to the social setting and the mother's personality. One fact which the writer found by hard experience was that, in her own particular area at least, it was a mistake to expect a separated or divorced woman or a widow, who had a home and other children of her own, to go through with adoption. Martha and Olive (p. 46) actually allowed their babies to be placed before they realised that they could not let them go, but others in this situation who talked of adoption until the time of the child's birth very quickly changed their minds afterwards. This seems at variance with Miss Yelloly's findings about the presence of other children in the home.

It is the most mature and balanced natural mother who is able to face honestly and with understanding the question: 'Can I be both mother and father to my baby?' and very often, answering in the negative, she will decide upon adoption as being in the best interests of her child. She will appreciate the basic difference between the home of an illegitimate child and an adoptive home: that whereas room has to be made for the illegitimate child in a family which is already complete without him, the adopted one steps into a place prepared for him in a family which was not complete until he arrived.

What if the child has the misfortune to be born with a club foot or congenital dislocation of the hip? Such babies have for too long been regarded as unadoptable, but it is now coming to be recognised that some adopters are prepared to accept the challenge of a handicapped child. Great efforts may be needed to find such people, and much more casework is entailed than in a straightforward placing, but these are the very children who are most in need of security, and therefore a serious attempt should be made to find suitable adopters. Many adoption agencies are still unwilling to place babies with a history of mental illness, and here again there may be room for greater flexibility of policy. Rose's child was regarded as unadoptable because her father had marked schizophrenic tendencies. She took this very badly indeed, and her overflowing anger against her own father and the baby's father was extended to men in general, especially the paediatrician.[2]

The parting

Sooner or later, with varying amounts of help from the social worker and almost always with some degree of pain to the mother, the decision for adoption is made and preparations begin. The mother will already know in broad outline how the adoption process is carried out, for she will have been told this when considering with the social worker the various alternatives open to her. The details will vary according to the locality. In the writer's area the Adoption Society was an independent voluntary organisation whose office was in a large city two hours' journey away. This, although costly in travelling time, had one great advantage: babies from the worker's area were placed with adopters in and around the town, and in the same way adopters in the area were offered babies whose mothers lived in the city, so that the risk of chance meeting between the two was very small indeed.

Adoption placings may also be made through the local authority Children's Department, and a number of diocesan Moral and Social Welfare Councils have an adoption agency as part of their casework service for unmarried parents. In addition, voluntary organisations such as Dr Barnardo's Homes or the Children's Society can be extremely helpful when the mother is uncertain about parting with the child, or if there is doubt about his fitness for adoption.

Private arrangements and third-party placings also still occur frequently, although the risks entailed are usually thought to be greater. Good adoption work demands insight, knowledge and skill of a high degree, and it is the aim of a registered agency to provide these.

Whatever the administrative setting, there is always an application form asking for the names, addresses, ages and marital status of the parents and other particulars. Filling in this form will perhaps be the first practical step the mother has to take, and will begin the process of offering her child for adoption. She should be encouraged to see to this and other practical matters for herself as far as possible, as part of the process of helping her to grow in maturity and responsibility. She will perhaps take her baby to the clinic for his medical examination. In many Mother and Baby Homes she is encouraged to prepare a full layette for the child to take with him to his new home. This is sometimes regarded as a waste of the mother's scarce resources, since the adopters will have made great preparations for his arrival. Here again it is a mistake to have an inflexible rule, but most mothers who love their babies are comforted by the thought that they sent him away well equipped, and moreover the carefully knitted woollies and snowy napkins are tangible evidence to the adopters that their baby has been cherished before he came to them. Also it may help the more thoughtless and irresponsible mother if she is encouraged to provide as much as she can. Some mothers offer a toy, a prayer-book or a Bible with a plea that it be given to the child when he is old enough to understand. She must be told clearly that this is entirely at the discretion of the new parents, but many good adopters willingly agree.

It will also help the mother if she is making plans for her own life after she leaves hospital or the Mother and Baby Home. Perhaps she is returning home; who will be there to welcome her? She may arrange a short holiday before starting work again: in the same job, or something quite different? Short periods away from the Home may be necessary while she looks for work or lodgings, and these will help to prepare her for the break with her baby.

The case committee of the adoption agency will require the fullest medical and social information about the baby and his parents. Obviously it is best if this is prepared by the long-term caseworker whom the mother knows and trusts, rather than that she should have to tell her story all over again to an adoption worker. Moreover, it is either the social worker in the Mother and Baby Home or the long-term caseworker who has the task of assembling the various documents needed: the mother's application form, the preliminary consent slip from the memorandum describing the adoption process which is required to be given to her, the two medical cartificates (one neo-natal and one at six weeks old) and in particular the results of the Wassermann reaction test for venereal disease and the phenylketonuria test for mental handicap. In addition to these, at the actual handing over of the baby there will be required the child's full-length birth certificate, a diet sheet, milk token books, medical card and the mother's signed consent to vaccination, immunisation and any necessary medical treatment for the baby. The mother must do as much as she can for herself and in any case should be kept in touch with the progress of the adoption arrangements. She should be informed as soon as a date is arranged for the transfer of the baby, and also be told, if she wishes, a certain amount about the prospective adopters.

Naturally, no details which could lead to their identification will be supplied, but the mother may usually know the occupation of the adopting father, what sort of house they live in and whether they have any other children, so that she is able to build up a mental picture of her baby's future home. One young mother was very anxious that her child should have grandparents living near at hand and was happy to be told that her son would have not only grandparents but a very active great-grandmother.

Many caseworkers have found from experience that it is nearly always helpful to both sides if the adopters meet the mother of the child for a few minutes, if she desires this and they also are willing, either at the handing-over of the baby or shortly beforehand. From the mother's point of view, the advantage of this is that it makes her baby's future life much more of a reality to her. It is good that her caseworker can assure her that her baby will be loved and cherished, but very much more convincing if she can actually see the people who are going to bring him up. Many a girl who was tempted to recall her baby has, in fact, held back from doing so because she 'couldn't disappoint his new parents, they were such nice people'. It is sometimes objected that it would be disastrous if the girl did not like the adopters, but in practice this happens very seldom. It should be stressed that the meeting is a voluntary one on both sides; and moreover if the adopters and the baby have been carefully matched, it is not likely that the adults concerned will be strongly incompatible. In one instance, where the adoptive mother had a marked facial disfigurement, the girl's caseworker was told of this and the girl was discouraged from asking for a meeting.

This encounter is inevitably an emotional ordeal, and the caseworker must remain firmly in control throughout. Very often the adoptive father plays a major part, and it is he, even more than the new mother, who can comfort and reassure the girl. From the adopters' point of view, besides giving them insight into the early life of their baby, this brief glimpse of the mother can be valuable years later when the child is curious about his origins. It will carry a great deal of weight with him if they can say, for example: 'We did see your mother for a few minutes. She was tall and slender, with straight dark hair and she had on a pretty red dress. She cried when she said "goodbye" to you, but we told her how much we loved you already.'

Good management is essential if the traumatic experience of transferring a baby from one mother to another is to be fruitful for all concerned. Two workers and three rooms are required. Usually the girl and her caseworker will be in one room, the prospective adopters in another. The girl will be gently invited to give her baby to her own caseworker, who will hand him to her colleague; she herself will not leave the girl at any time. The baby is shown to the adopters, who have him to themselves for a few minutes if they have not seen him before. When they have accepted him, if the mother wishes to see them the child is removed from the room before she is brought in. The meeting is just long enough for the adopters to thank and reassure her, and the actual parting is over. It helps a great deal if the operation is carried out smoothly, without haste or anxious searching for missing documents, and in particular the mother should never be asked at this late stage whether she wishes to change her mind and keep the baby. If the preliminary casework has been well done there is no need for such a question, and at this stage in particular the worker must concentrate on supporting and strengthening her client to carry out what is almost certainly the most crucial decision she has ever had to make.

Short-term fostering

Every casework agency for unmarried parents should collect, and take good care of, its own battalion of foster-parents who are able to offer family care to a baby on discharge from hospital, until such time as he is placed for adoption at the age of six or eight weeks. The fostering service is an integral part of the agency's function, and its quality is important in the first place because the foster-parents accept the responsibility of caring for an individual baby in the first few weeks of his life, and secondly because their attitude may have a strong influence on the mother if she visits the child. Many agencies, and individual social workers, seem to take their foster-homes too much for granted, expecting them always to be able to take a baby at short notice and look after him well with the minimum amount of consideration. In fact the foster-mother, although she is paid for what she does, is carrying out one of the most useful functions of a voluntary social worker, and like all such workers she gives much better service if she is trained and thus enabled to co-operate effectively. She should have some insight into the problems of unmarried parenthood, and also a degree of understanding of what happens to the baby after he leaves her care – a question which is naturally of great concern to her. Group discussions attended by half a dozen foster-mothers would be most valuable for this purpose. Some foster-mothers feel almost as bereft as the natural mother when the baby is placed with adopters, and it has on occasions proved an excellent plan to let the foster-mother herself put the baby into the arms of the adoptive mother and tell her of the infant's individual likes and dislikes. The foster-mother cannot give the child real security unless she has peace of mind about his future, and moreover a painful parting will make her less willing to undertake the care of another baby.

The best foster-homes are those in which the mother not only has a love of small babies and some experience in looking after them, but also has the ungrudging support of her husband in spite of disturbed nights and alterations in daily routine. The growing sons and daughters welcome the baby, too, and although parting with the first child is usually a saddening experience, the whole family gradually develops the detachment that is the essential counter-weight to the love they give to their small visitor.

When the mother decides not to look after her baby herself, he must either be placed for adoption on discharge from hospital or fostered. Because the worker has specialised knowledge, the decision as to which plan to follow will be mainly her responsibility. From the point of view of both the adopters and the baby, John Bowlby is probably right when he says that it is unmistakably 'in the interests of the adopted baby's mental health for him to be adopted soon after birth',[3] but there are risks in this as well as practical difficulties. Baby Keith was placed with Mr and Mrs Gray at ten days old as an apparently normal baby, but after ten weeks of increasing difficulty and anxiety, they asked for him to be withdrawn on account of both physical and mental disability. This would almost certainly have been discernible if he had had a routine pre-placement medical examination at the age of six weeks. The risk of recall by the mother is probably no greater in early adoption, provided there has been time for adequate casework beforehand, but it does involve choosing suitable adopters, and finalising arrangements, for a baby who is not yet born. Hence a limited period in the care of a loving and capable foster-mother has much to recommend it. The infant's physical and – to some extent – mental progress can be assessed, the mother has a chance to make sure that she can surrender the child, and there is time to plan the placing of the baby for adoption with the care that should always mark so important a step.

If the mother has made a firm decision for adoption, the separation will come when she and her child leave hospital and go their different ways; she will not usually visit her baby while he is in the care of foster-parents. But if the child's future is still uncertain she may wish to see him from time to time. Under these circumstances mature and sympathetic foster-parents can be immensely helpful. The mother is more than likely to discuss her predicament with them, and the mere fact that they are *not* trained social workers, but ordinary sensible people, will lend great weight to the views they are likely to express about what she should do.

A common practical difficulty about fostering arrangements is financial. It is generally agreed that foster-parents ought to be adequately paid for the valuable work they do, but the adoption agencies very rarely have funds available for this purpose and few unmarried mothers are able to afford three or four pounds a week for two months. Sometimes the putative father is able to contribute, but failing this, the Supplementary Benefits Commission will usually consider favourably an application for a special grant to make up the mother's maternity allowance to the required sum.[4]

The mother after the parting

The mother who has offered her baby to prospective adopters is very often in the full sense a bereaved mother, however realistic and unselfish her decision may have been. She will talk of him entirely in the past tense, for the brief episode of his life with her is ended as completely as though he had indeed died. 'He always woke up at three o'clock in the morning', 'he had a funny crinkle in his right ear', she will say. Her need of supportive help during this period is just as great as it was during the first stages of her pregnancy, but very different in its nature. At that time she was in a state of anxiety and fear; now she feels loss and sorrow, and she needs to be allowed her time of mourning, for she is likely to go through all the stages associated with actual bereavement. A first phase of numbness from shock will be broken into more and more frequently by moments of strong longing for her baby, and this desire is quite often embodied in physical pain in the arms, breasts or abdomen. She may wake suddenly from sleep thinking she heard the child cry, and grope for the cot that is not there. It is at this stage that the wish to recall the baby is most compelling. Gradually, over a varying period of time the pangs lessen in intensity, but for months afterwards the mother may feel an urge to look into every pram she sees in search of her own baby, and may either compulsively handle small children or avoid them altogether.

When her family and friends understand this reaction their sympathy will help her to encounter and grow through it, but in fact the intensity of her loss is seldom realised. The worker should be at pains to prepare the grandparents for their daughter's return home, and to ensure that she is given time to mourn. Too often she is expected to take up the threads of normal life again as though nothing had happened. The caseworker is sometimes her only safety-valve. In her care of the mother who has offered her baby for adoption, the caseworker's objective is to enable her client to accept the separation, not negatively as a renunciation on her own part but as a positive action which she performed for her child's sake. This is most necessary for her future mental health and peace of mind. Unfortunately it is often the very client who is most in need of help in this respect who is least willing to receive it: the emotionally immature girl often instinctively represses the thoughts that cause her pain. She should be gently helped to express freely her thoughts, desires and memories of her baby, whatever they may be, for only so can she learn to live with them.

The caseworker will stress the constructive aspects of the situation, especially the child's security in the love of two parents, and she may be able to reinforce this with a favourable report from the adoption caseworker who is visiting him in his new home. Also she will encourage the girl to make and carry out plans for her own future whenever she shows any capacity for this, in training for a better sort of job, attending evening classes or perhaps leaving her parents' house and setting up her own home. As in the first interview, she will avoid facile reassurances of the 'don't worry, you'll soon get over it' kind. Brenda's (p. 11) worker suggested to her that one day she would be very likely to have a husband and other babies whom she would be able to love and cherish. Brenda looked up and said, quietly but very firmly, 'Miss X, one child will *never* make up for another.'[5]

It is true that homecoming marks a turning-point which many girls look forward to with eagerness for weeks beforehand, and they themselves may be quite unprepared for the intensity of their reaction to parting with the baby, unless they are forewarned by the caseworker. They will spend the first weeks at home in a confused emotional state, between grief for the baby and relief at the end of the episode. The return to normal life is often the best cure for the sorrow once the acute stage is over, and it is better if the mother starts work again as soon as she is fit. A long period of unemployment and idleness has a markedly depressing effect, and should be avoided whenever possible. The caseworker will, if necessary, help her client to find a congenial job as well as offering her friendship and support for as long as the girl desires it.[6]

According to the records of one adoption society, about three babies out of every hundred placed with adopters are recalled by their mothers, usually during the first two weeks of acute grief, but sometimes after the legal consent form has been signed. Even the most careful and thorough casework cannot always prevent this. A frequent cause is that the mother has resumed her relationship with the child's father, and so her hopes of marrying him have revived, however unrealistically. The caseworker must first of all satisfy herself that this is not just an emotional swing on the mother's part, and she will probably confront the mother with all the practical difficulties that will face her if she recalls her baby, as well as exploring her deeper motives for doing so.

June was nineteen, and lived with her mother, who had heart disease, and her fairly active grandmother who ruled the household with an iron rod. Her parents had been divorced when she was five. Her boy-friend, Will, was a labourer at the foundry, and when her pregnancy was discovered Granma promptly sent her away to a Mother and Baby Home. When baby Stewart was placed with adopters, June returned. Nothing was altered; Granma gave her a lecture about behaving better in future, and forbade her to mention her baby. When the time came for her to be interviewed by the guardian *ad litem*, the Children's Officer came to the factory where June worked. Thus taken off her guard, June wept bitterly and said she wanted her baby back, but by the time her caseworker arrived to see her at home she had recovered her composure and said she knew it was best for Stewart to stay where he was: the guardian *ad litem*, however, provoked the same reaction on his second visit, and this time June went home and told her grandmother that she was having Stewart back. Granma forbade her to bring the child to her house; June found lodgings in a shabby street near to her boy-friend's home. As she had already signed her legal consent to Stewart's adoption it was necessary for herself and Will to appear before the magistrates to ask for his return, but this was granted, as it nearly always is. The child legally belongs to his mother until the moment when the adoption order is made, and however precarious the mother's plans may be, the Magistrates or the County Court Judge very seldom refuse her application. Here is another instance in which the legal concept of 'possession' of a child by his parents does not always work out for the child's good. Stewart and his father and mother led a most precarious existence for at least two years. Their marriage was delayed because June's grandmother discouraged her mother from giving her consent, and they moved from place to place in an unsuccessful search for decent living accommodation and adequately paid work for Will.

Sometimes the mother's recall of the child from adoptive parents is justifiable, as when the father hears belatedly of the baby's birth and marriage is then decided upon. However sympathetic the caseworker may feel towards the disappointment of the adopters and whatever her views as to the wisdom of the recall, she will nevertheless be ready to acknowledge the new situation and help her client to make the best possible arrangements for care of the baby, including, perhaps an application for an affiliation order.

When the adopters have had the child in their care for a full three months, they can apply either to the Juvenile Court or to the County Court for the adoption order which transfers to them all parental rights and responsibilities towards the child. At the hearing of the application a prescribed form of consent signed by the mother must be produced, but apart from the provision in the Adoption Act, 1950, that the child must be at least six weeks old, there is no definite ruling as to the time when she signs this document, and the policy of adoption agencies varies in regard to it. Some will ask the mother to sign it within a few days of placing the baby, and others withhold the form until the full three months have elapsed, on the grounds that the mother must have all the time she is legally allowed in which to change her mind. When is the best time to deal with it from the mother's point of view is a moot point. She cannot but feel that this document marks a decisive step, since her signature on it must be witnessed by a magistrate or Clerk to the Justices, and this involves a certain ceremony although there is in fact nothing irrevocable about it; she can still apply to the Court to get her baby back, as we have seen.

Most mothers, however, are acutely conscious that the consent form marks their final relinquishing of the baby, and some will be glad to have the full three months before they take this step, but many others find this transaction a painful reopening of the wound of separation after it has begun to heal, and would rather get it over quickly. Most Children's Departments are in favour of fairly early completion of the consent form, because this enables them to have the necessary documents assembled in good time, and so avoids delay in the making of the Order. The caseworker should use such discretion as she is allowed in such a way that the mother signs the form when she feels ready to do so, whether early or late.

It might be more satisfactory if the mother were to vest her consent in the adoption agency when the child is placed, so that if all goes well she is not approached again, except that she would be notified of the date of the hearing of the application. She would still be free to reclaim her baby if she decided to do so, as she is at present, but she would be spared the anguish of being asked once again if she had really made up her mind. A system similar to this is in operation in some American States.

Before the Order is made the mother must still be interviewed by the guardian *ad litem*, who is specially appointed to look after the interests of mother and child, and must satisfy him that she has freely offered her baby for adoption. As the story of June has already shown, this can produce some difficult situations especially when the mother is frank enough to say flatly that she was *not* willing to give up her child and only did so 'because my dad wouldn't have him at home'.

The granting of the Adoption Order marks the end of the unmarried girl's status as a mother, and by the time this stage is reached her restoration as a normal member of the community should be almost complete. Some agencies are willing to ask the adopters for a photograph of the child at this stage as a final gift to the mother, and a certain number of girls find this a help, but many more reject the offer because, as Deborah (p. 111) said: 'Whenever I felt depressed I'd get the photograph out and have a good cry over it, and it wouldn't do me any good.'

What is the final outcome? What does it do to a girl to have an illegitimate baby and give him to adopters? Very few indeed come through this process completely unchanged. For some it is an enriching and maturing experience to have another person so completely dependent on them, and to be responsible for planning his future. Moreover they learn from their suffering a profound sympathy with other people in adversity, and the ability to help them in a very practical, down-to-earth way. Sometimes it marks the end of adolescence and the beginning of adult life. For the older woman it can provide a painfully transient and yet deeply satisfying experience of motherhood. The very young mother, especially, may try to represss her memories of the ordeal. Psychiatrists see many such casualties.[7] Some may be filled with guilt in later life; some will become embittered and aggressive, others deeply distrustful and timid. Very many are, at least for a time, at risk because they are profoundly insecure after parting from their babies, and their desperate need for a loving, protective relationship too often results in a second pregnancy or a very quick marriage.

For many a girl there is a period of transition while she is getting her grip on normal life again. This usually means going back to the same outward circumstances – to life at home with Mum and Dad – but feeling herself to be a very different person as a result of her experience. There will be interaction between the new self and the familiar routine, each seeking to change the other. The tragedy is that the dead weight of habit so often stifles the awakened instincts and blots out the glimpsed possibility of a fuller life, so that the new self must either rebel or capitulate into dull acquiescence. There are few more saddening experiences for the caseworker than to find that her young client, who during her pregnancy was so full of plans for 'afterwards', has sunk into complete apathy under the monotony of factory work and the Friday night dance. Whether she should try to prevent this apparent capitulation, and how, is a question bordering on the philosophical and outside the scope of this book.

It is clear that follow-up casework can be of great importance, but how long the individual client keeps in touch with her worker depends largely on her own personality and circumstances. Sometimes the relationship has remained on a basically impersonal footing throughout; nothing more than practical help has been asked for, and when the need for this is ended the connection is automatically severed. Sometimes the worker's presence evokes too many memories of a painful experience which has not been fully accepted, and the mother will avoid seeing the worker if she can. In other instances a more enduring relationship will have been formed, and although the caseworker's underlying purpose is always to enable her client to cope with her own life and problems more effectually for herself, it is usually a mistake for her to discourage the girl who continues to drop in at the office to discuss her personal problems. She is almost certainly still in need of emotional support in some degree.

Administration should certainly not impose a time limit, and whenever the final interview comes the client should be left with a warm assurance that she is welcome to return at any time, with or without a problem.

8. Keeping the Baby

The first adjustments

Dorothy (p. 27) was typical of many immature, emotionally stunted girls in her insistence on keeping her baby, but it does not follow from this that all unmarried mothers who decide to bring up their children themselves are inadequate or unbalanced. Miss M. (p. 32), who was a mature and responsible woman, made her decision in full awareness of the price she would have to pay, and for her child's sake was prepared to leave her home town, give up most of her friends and face alone whatever problems might arise. Kathleen (p. 34) was so full of maternal love that the difficulties she was likely to encounter in bringing up both Peter and his baby sister carried little weight with her, but she was an excellent housewife and mother and had a basically happy and equable temperament.

Moreover, there is no doubt that many girls who keep their babies are sincerely devoted to their children and make excellent mothers. The trouble is that society often loads the dice against them so heavily that they have no chance of bringing up their children happily and successfully.

The girl who has decided to bring up her child herself is in a very different situation from the mother who is preparing for adoption, and the casework approach is different, too. Instead of leading up to a single dramatic event when the baby is placed for adoption and helping her to recover afterwards, the unmarried mother's whole life assumes a new direction and a new purpose. The caseworker can help her in this. Does the girl realise that her new existence will be to a large extent child-centred? Is she prepared for the implications of this in domestic clutter and broken nights, baby-sitting and less money to spend? How will she be able to sustain her role as mother after the novelty of it has worn off, and her charming baby has grown into a destructive two-year-old? Without being discouraging, the worker must help her client to be realistic about the nature and quality of her future daily life.

In the case of the girl who is keeping her baby it is abundantly true, as Rose Bernstein suggests, that her experience of pregnancy and childbirth should be made as satisfying as possible.[1] She may be encouraged to breast-feed the child and to take the fullest responsibility for his care, and in doing this she may mature quite rapidly, showing qualities of reliability and initiative which were not evident before the child was born.

Are social workers sometimes too exacting in their standards when they assess an unmarried mother's ability to look after her child? We tend to judge them by our own ideas of what a mother should be like, and this seems to imply selflessness and practical ability of a high order. 'Cats make better mothers!' used to be cruelly said of a nursery full of unwilling and diffident girls struggling to put their wriggling babies through the routine of nappies and bottles. It surely would be more realistic to ask: How does this girl's performance as an unmarried mother differ from what could be expected of her if she were married? She would almost certainly receive less criticism and more encouragement if she had a ring on her finger.

Moreover, social workers are acutely conscious that the unmarried mother who has decided to keep her baby is preparing to bring up a socially handicapped child. She, therefore, needs to be an especially good mother to make up for this; it is felt that she needs understanding both of the normal stages of child development and of the particular difficulties she is likely to encounter. Obviously it would be absurd to attempt to give her a packaged course in child psychology, but she can at least be helped to see the importance of a settled but flexible routine, and consistency, in a loving relationship, during the early stages. One of the advantages of a few weeks in a Mother and Baby Home is that the young mother has the opportunity to discuss with other girls in the same situation, and with experienced workers, the problems that lie before her.

Financial arrangements

The most immediate of these problems are practical and economic. She and her child must have somewhere to live and adequate means of support, or their life together will never become a reality at all. Too many unmarried mothers are compelled to give up the struggle to keep their child for lack of suitable living accommodation and inability to make ends meet. A crisis point may be reached after anything between six months and as many years of frequent moves and increasing difficulty, which embitter the mother and destroy the child's sense of security, so that when he is finally received into the care of a local authority or voluntary organisation he may be already markedly disturbed. The caseworker must do everything possible to prevent this by helping the mother to make satisfactory arrangements, whether in her parents' home or elsewhere, at the start.

The Social Security maternity grant, which at the time of writing is £22, and the maternity allowance of £4 10*s* weekly for eighteen weeks beginning eleven weeks before confinement, make it possible for the mother who has been in regular employment to provide the first necessities for her baby, and if she does not qualify for this the Supplementary Benefits Commission will usually make a comparable grant. Finally, it remains to be seen whether the putative father will help financially.

It is unfortunate that this often appears to be the first and only time that he comes into the picture. In actual fact, as we have seen, he is unlikely to be helpful unless he is at least able to show some degree of concern for the girl and their child, and thus it is doubly mistaken to approach him simply as a possible source of money. There are, however, two recognised ways in which he can contribute.

Private agreements and affiliation orders

The parents of an illegitimate child can come to an agreement whereby the father contributes a stipulated sum for the child's maintenance. A solicitor will draw up a legal contract providing for this, or alternatively one of the printed forms supplied for the purpose by the National Council for the Unmarried Mother and her Child may be used. This states that the mother and the man whom she 'alleges is the father of the child' mutually agree that he will make to her a weekly payment which after deduction of tax will amount to a stated sum, and that this arrangement shall continue, unless the child dies or is adopted, until he is sixteen years of age. When this document has been signed by both parents, it should be stamped by the Board of Inland Revenue, at a cost which varies from 4*s* 3*d* to 10*s* 6*d* depending on the amount of the weekly payment, and is then legally enforceable in the County Court.

This type of agreement has the great advantage of privacy. It can be completed by the parents themselves if they wish, but more often the caseworker acts as negotiator, and payments under it are frequently made through her. In this case she will keep an independent account of all sums received from the father and forwarded by her to the mother, and thus there is no need for a continuation of direct contact between the parents. If the remittances from the father fall into arrears the worker can find out the reasons for this without the emotional involvement that the mother would feel, and she can conduct the periodical review of the amount paid which is provided for in the agreement. An agreement signed by both parents, even if it is never honoured, can be used as evidence in an application for an affiliation order, and if the father has made any payment under it, would be regarded as proof of his acceptance of paternity.

Private agreements have two main disadvantages, however. The first is that income tax arrangements are somewhat complicated. The amount to be paid is expressed as a net figure after deduction of tax, and the father has to supply periodical certificates of deduction of tax so that the mother can reclaim the child's tax allowance. This is a slow and tedious process. If the father fails to send the certificate the refund of tax is delayed, and in any case the arrangement makes difficulties for a mother who has a weekly budget.

The other drawback is the difficulty of enforcing payments if they fall into arrears. This involves bringing an action for debt in the County Court, and although the costs of such an action would be added to the debt they have to be paid by the mother in the first place. Moreover, as it is now proposed to abolish committal proceedings for debt there appears to be no final compulsion on the father to meet his commitments.

If there is doubt about the ability or the willingness of the father to make regular payments under a private agreement, an affiliation order is preferable. This is made on the application of the mother to the Magistrates under the Affiliation Proceedings Act, 1957, and involves taking out a summons against the putative father. This must normally be done within a year of the child's birth, but if he has contributed to the child's maintenance the application may be made within twelve months of the last payment. If the father is abroad, information may be lodged with the Clerk to the Justices, and the summons will be served on his return to this country. But a great deal of careful casework is needed before the summons is applied for, because it is a waste of time for the mother to appear unless she has convincing proof of the paternity of the man she names. Experience suggests that it is the lack of this, even more than the publicity involved, which accounts for the comparatively small proportion of women who apply for affiliation orders.[2] It is a common occurrence for a girl to have an intimate relationship with a man unknown to anyone except perhaps a friend or workmate who can only say that they were 'going around together'. There is no witness when she tells her lover of her pregnancy, and he may retire from the scene without writing to her or giving her any money. In these circumstances there is complete absence of any of the three items of proof which will be accepted by the court: an admission of paternity by the alleged father in the presence of a third person, letters referring to the pregnancy which clearly imply responsibility, or any gift to the child or payment for his maintenance.

It is the concern of the caseworker to ascertain how much evidence the mother can produce in support of her claim. The compilation of a detailed history of the relationship may demand much time and patience.

'When did you first go out with Tommy?'

'Well, I remember it was on a Thursday because I always get home late on Thursdays.'

'Can you remember which Thursday it was?'

'No, but it was raining.'

'What did you do? You went to the pictures? What did you see? *The Sound of Music?*' This particular film ran for six months, so it is no use going to the public library to look up the cinema advertisements in back numbers of the local paper. The possibilities are better when a parent or friend has been to see the young man concerned and can affirm that he undertook to 'pay for it', and if the girl has not yet told her boy-friend of her condition she may be advised to do so in the presence of someone else who will act as a witness.

The worker herself should avoid being called as a witness in affiliation applications, for this destroys the impartiality which is essential to her proper functioning as a caseworker. When she interviews the putative father she should be most careful to make it clear to him that although she will not willingly give evidence against him, she can nevertheless be subpoenaed to appear in court. Fortunately, in practice this seldom happens.

If the mother can produce a reasonable amount of corroboration, an appointment is made for her to see the agency's honorary solicitor, who will act for her when her application is heard. He may decide to write to the putative father and await a reply from him before the date of the hearing is arranged and a summons taken out, and will arrange for legal aid if the mother is eligible for this.

The case will not be heard before the birth of the child, but if the Order is made within six weeks after, the payments may start from the date of birth. Otherwise they are due from the day on which the Order is made. The public are excluded from the hearing, but even so the Court appearance is often an ordeal for the mother. She is summoned for the start of the session at 10.30 a.m., but the cases to be heard in a closed Court are nearly always put last on the list, so that she has to spend weary hours in waiting for her turn. It usually helps a great deal if the worker is present to explain what is happening in these unfamiliar surroundings, and perhaps to sit with her client while a case is being heard in open Court in order that she may watch the administration of the oath and the giving of evidence. The worker will in any case have prepared the girl in advance, so that she understands the procedure of the Court and can answer questions clearly and firmly. Even so, the mother may have a difficult time, for it sometimes happens that her former boy-friend may deny all responsibility and even produce other young men to swear that they also have had intercourse with her. If he admits paternity, however, it is merely a question of deciding how much he is to pay.

A blood test is sometimes demanded by a man named as a putative father. A child inherits the blood group of one or other of his parents, and so, if he proves to have blood of a group which is neither his mother's nor that of the man named, it is clear that he cannot be the father. The usual type of blood test cannot indicate more than this, and moreover it cannot prove that a particular man is responsible because there are countless other men with the same blood group, but it is sometimes a help in resolving doubts about paternity.

The first payment is due at the magistrates' clerk's office seven days after the Order is made, but it may be a month before the mother receives any money, especially if costs have to be paid first. The magistrates' clerk will do what he can to enforce the Order, issuing a summons after three weeks of default, but it quite often happens that the man responsible disappears and arrears mount up. If he is sent to prison for non-payment the mother is no better off. Since the Maintenance Orders Act of 1958 it is possible to have the amount payable under an affiliation order deducted from the putative father's wages or salary, but the courts seem slow to make use of their powers in this respect, and in any case it is easy for the man to change his job.

The unmarried mother who chooses not to return to work, but to look after her child while he is young, can apply to the Supplementary Benefits Commission for an allowance, which will be paid according to her circumstances. The Commission's officers are, however, bound to do what they can to get the father to maintain his child. As they have access to the records of the National Insurance Department they are sometimes able to trace a man who has gone away to work in another part of the country. The Supplementary Benefits Commission will not divulge his address, but as they are usually prepared to forward letters from the mother, this can on occasions be a great help in establishing contact with a man who may have had a panic reaction to the news of his paternity. The Commission sometimes brings pressure to bear upon a mother who is unwilling to take the father of her child to court; this is not necessarily harmful, as it may compel her to come to terms with her confused feelings about him, but her reluctance may be increased by the knowledge that as long as she remains on Supplementary Benefit her income will be augmented by only a few shillings a week from her affiliation order or private agreement, whereas if she goes back to work she will not only have a higher income from her earnings, but will receive the full benefit of the maintenance payments as well. This hard economic fact is responsible for many mothers' returning to work earlier than they would otherwise have done. And even so, the number of unmarried mothers who can earn enough to keep themselves and their babies without any help at all, in the form of houseroom with their parents or an allowance from the father of their baby, is very small indeed.

Under special circumstances various voluntary organisations such as Dr Barnardo's Homes, the Children's Society or the Buttle Trust may be approached for help, but what they can do is strictly limited when the mother is receiving Supplementary Benefit. Mrs Green, for instance, when she was living on her widow's pension and what she earned by daily cleaning work, had an allowance of £2 per week from a voluntary source for the maintenance of her illegitimate grandson, whereas Ethel, who was mentally and physically disabled and whose father was unfit for work, received only 15*s* because there was a considerable sum in Supplementary Benefit going into the house. Once a child is on the books of a voluntary society, however, they will provide most valuable help with clothing, holidays, school trips and other extra expenses as long as the need for help continues.[3]

Learning the new role

The arrival of every first-born child opens a new chapter in the life experience of his mother. When she has no wedding-ring on her finger her joy at his birth is in conflict with a whole array of other emotions, and in particular her attitude to the baby is coloured by her relationship with his father. The caseworker can do a great deal to help the girl to sort out and acknowledge her feelings about him. There may be a physical likeness in the child which recalls vividly the young man who has jilted her, or perhaps she is unwilling to trace in the baby any resemblance to his father because she has rejected him, and as time goes on she may try to suppress any traits which remind her of the father. On the other hand she may have a continuing relationship with her lover which may be strengthened or altered by the child's birth, but which in any case is likely to be ambivalent in some degree.

These feelings will influence the decision about the child's future, as has already been pointed out. It is not suggested that a mother who keeps her baby should necessarily remain on intimate terms with his father. It is probably better for everyone concerned if she does not. What is important is that she should neither transfer to the child her own feelings about the man, nor repress them. It is not only embarrassment but often a great degree of resentment and bitterness that impels her to shut him out of the situation. The caseworker can be useful in getting her to acknowledge and release these feelings, by reminding her that her boy-friend is as much a father as she a mother, and that this is important to him. If she can concede his right to see the child when he is going to help to maintain him, it will be better for her own peace of mind as well as producing a healthier atmosphere for the child to grow up in.

Quite apart from her feelings about her partner, the situation is complicated enough. As she looks at her baby she may feel shame at his very existence, or at her own conduct, and she may cover this with defiance of the whole world which she imagines to be attacking her, or assume an attitude of hard indifference to what other people think, or be fiercely over-protective of her child. A further complication is that every attitude of mind finds its own justification, so that the girl who is on the watch for criticism will perceive it where none was intended, and the aggressive mother will constantly encounter threats.

At all events the unmarried girl is extremely vulnerable when she first arrives home with her baby. Whenever possible, the caseworker will have prepared the family for her return, helping the grandparents to understand what the new situation will be like. They know their daughter well enough, certainly, but are they prepared for her to be perhaps a bit authoritarian about baby management? She will be to some degree unsure of herself in her new role as a mother, and may need their tolerance. It is fortunate that she very often receives a friendly welcome from the community which helps her to relax her defensiveness. In this, as in everything else, the interplay between her inner self and the outside world is close and complicated. The caseworker's sympathy and insight can help her to adjust to her new role as a handicapped mother. It is not overstating the case to call her this, although the degree of disability will vary according to her temperament and social circumstances. The first time she takes her baby down the street in his pram may require an act of courage on her part, and the second time her attitude will be coloured by her experiences on the first occasion. Even the very young mother who is regarded as a bit of a heroine by her own friends when she returns from a Mother and Baby Home has to be absorbed into the circle again, and she, perhaps especially, has to learn to accept a different status in the group. Jennifer is back home again, certainly, but it is a changed Jennifer, because she has brought her baby son Simon with her. The welcome home is soon over, the novelty soon wears off, but Simon comes to the teething stage, grows out of his clothes, crawls into the cupboards. It is inevitable that his mother's relationship with the outside world will be reflected in her attitude towards him. If she is at odds with her parents it is at bottom because of Simon. So she may lose her temper when he cries in the night, and the next morning may angrily refuse to let her mother pick him up. Simon himself is well aware of the tension between them, and may act out his fear and anxiety.

It takes an almost superhuman self-knowledge and self-control to avoid this sort of chain reaction, but the caseworker who has known Jennifer since the early days of her pregnancy can perform valuable service as a safety-valve for the release of tension, especially if she can offer, at the right moment, the blessed relief of a sense of humour. But how can Jennifer be both mother and father to her son? In actual fact she cannot, because it takes two people to offer the duality of tenderness and strength, of immediate and long-term caring, that is the essence of the parental relationship. There should whenever possible be a father-figure in the child's world, perhaps Grandfather or an uncle. But his mother's attitude towards men in general is likely to be greatly affected by her status. She may be shy and diffident, bitter, defensive, aggressive, provoking; she is almost certain to meet men who will make offensive remarks to her or assume that she is good for an evening's pleasure, simply because she is an unmarried mother. Her reaction to this will depend upon her psychological make-up, but for many girls there is a strong temptation, relating to her equivocal position in the community, to 'give 'em something to talk about'.

In the end it is the sense of being separate, of being different from everyone else, that most unmarried mothers find hardest to bear. Somehow Jennifer must face and accept all this, for herself, without letting it have an adverse effect upon her child. She will be lonely, but must not expect Simon to be company for her; he will have his own friends and his own interests. She must not tie him to her apron-strings, but encourage him to go out into the world. She needs a considerable degree of detachment if she is to sustain her difficult role. Instead of this it often happens that she embarks upon a desperate and unrealistic search for a man who will marry her and take care of her and her son, and this unfortunately exposes her to a strong risk of a second pregnancy. In this situation the caseworker has a part to play, not only as an accessible person who has time to listen, although this is in itself important, but also to help the unmarried mother to make her life as full and satisfying as possible. It is worth some trouble to ensure that her job is congenial as well as adequately paid.

Sometimes it is helpful to introduce her to another girl in the same situation as herself, although skill and discretion are needed in this. Since the ultimate object is always to help the natural mother to find a secure position in the community, it is often better to use the services provided by an outward-looking church congregation, or perhaps the Townswomen's Guild or a social club. The local Child Welfare Clinic can be a great place for making friends. But perhaps the most satisfactory outlet for the unmarried mother is an opportunity to show friendship or give service to someone else, and the more mature girls sometimes show great depth and intensity of concern for those in need of help. Youth organisations, Hospital Friends, the W.R.V.S. or the housebound old lady round the corner may benefit greatly from their help, and the mother in her turn can at last feel herself to be accepted because she is of use to somebody.

This was certainly the case with Joan A. (p. 33). As time passed her voluntary social service occupied her more and more fully, but this did not even begin until her daughter was five. In the earlier years she had countless difficulties, many of which arose from her own insecurity. She was so touchy about her child that she walked out of more than one job because of what she felt were disparaging remarks from workmates; she fell sick, she ran into debt, she met and rejected a dozen men. Throughout this period the social worker found jobs, found lodgings, gave references and acted as banker, intermediary, safety-valve and supporter. When Joan began to give an evening a week to the W.R.V.S. she relaxed a little, and thenceforth the two processes of service and relaxation supplemented each other. Joan will never be a calm, placid person, but at least she can now bear to live with herself – most of the time.

Denise was very different. At the time when her child was born she was sixteen, and her parents were awaiting divorce. Her three brothers lived with their father, Denise and her two sisters with their mother. She took her baby home, but she was not very maternal. Her mother looked after the child, although Denise drew Supplementary Benefit and refused to take a job. The social worker, well aware of the situation, continued to visit. One day she was told that Denise had not returned home the previous night, and after a search she found her in the home of her boy-friend, a young man who had made a disastrous marriage some eighteen months before and had gone back to live with his parents. His mother was quite indifferent to the situation, and Denise's mother said at first that she did not want her back although she refused to let the baby go. Denise's Supplementary Benefit was stopped on the grounds that she was co-habiting and therefore the young man could keep her, but in fact she received nothing from him. Lack of money and the fact that she was outstaying her welcome lent weight to the caseworker's suggestion that she should go home, but there was a great deal of work to be done with Denise, her mother and her sisters before the situation reached a precarious sort of stability, for there were many emotional and personal problems in the family.

The caseworker should make it clear that the child must know his real mother. It often seems so much easier at first to let him call his grandparents Mother and Father, and to think of his real mother as a big sister. But sooner or later he will learn the truth, and the effect of this in unhappiness and delinquency is often disastrous for the whole family. The mother should also be prepared in advance for the moment, which is bound to come, when her son realises that all his friends have a father, and asks why he hasn't got one too. This is crucial, because his whole future attitude to his illegitimate birth will spring from the answer he receives. Since it is impossible to put children off with lies for long, and immoral to try to do so, whatever he is told must be the truth so far as it goes; it should go no further than the child's question. 'Of course you've got a daddy, Simon. Every little boy has one,' conveys both biological truth and reassurance. 'Where is he, then?' is more difficult. Sooner or later the child should be told quite simply that although his parents loved one another very much, they are not married to one another and therefore they do not live together. The younger the child is, the more easily he will accept the situation, and it seems best that he should be enabled to do so long before the moral implications appear to him. His attitude will in any case be conditioned by that of the grown-ups around him, and in proportion as they have accepted the situation, so also will he.

There is a clear need for long-term help, and experience suggests that much more should be done in this way to assist unmarried mothers who keep their babies. It is regrettable that many workers have too big a caseload for them to be able to provide really adequate after-care for all who should have it, and hence it is often a question of using their available time and energy to the best purpose.

'There can be no satisfactory solution for the problem of illegitimacy except prevention. Once the illegitimate child is born he is by that fact "at risk" in a way which the child born in wedlock is not. And the inescapable tragedy is that the best we can do for him is only a second best.'[4]

Is there really nothing more that society can do? The question remains to be considered in the last chapter.

9. Looking to the Future

An out-of-wedlock child 'does not ask to be born', and as he grows up he will be aware that his parents have laid a heavy disability upon him. He is more than likely to feel himself to be a second-rate person, and even worse, a superfluous one whose very right to be alive is in question. Hence, although we no longer condemn his parent as bad or immoral, nevertheless we regard it as irresponsible behaviour on their part to produce a socially handicapped child. So we have altered our attitude somewhat: either they were careless and bungled the contraceptive precautions, or else they are psychiatric 'cases', driven to having a baby by unconscious urges. These views, although over-simplified, are at least more realistic than the earlier ones, but traces of the old punitive attitude still exist both in the law and in social provisions, just as traces of the old fear and anger remain in our emotional reactions.

How it turns out

The extent of the illegitimate child's handicap can in part be measured by facts and figures. A comparison of the Toronto Study made in 1943 with Alexina McWhinnie's recent work on adults who were adopted in childhood[1] indicates that the child born out of wedlock has no more than a 50 per cent chance of growing into a well-adjusted adult, whether he is adopted or brought up by his mother. Since there are estimated to be 360,000 illegitimate children in Britain, this is a serious situation. The death-rate among illegitimate babies is still one-third higher than that for those whose mothers are married, and the proportion of those brought before the court or received into the care of local authorities is also greater.[2 3 4] In addition, the illegitimate child's legal disabilities are considerable.

Every experienced caseworker can produce evidence of the effects on personality, even in adult life, of these handicaps on the illegitimate child. Mr Brown, for example, had a chip on his shoulder as big as a log because of the fact of his birth. Mr Gold, born illegitimate, later became an adoptive father. He said, 'I don't like to think of another child going through what I went through when I was a boy'. Not until he was happily married could he feel assured that he was accepted as a person in his own right. The idea that an illegitimate child cannot be baptized is still quite common, and is part of the fable, which obstinately survives, that he is somehow 'tainted' with the 'sin' of his parents.

From a practical point of view, the greatest hazard to the out-of-wedlock child and his mother is insecurity, caused by lack of money and accommodation. The very child who has extra need of stability in his home and upbringing to compensate for his lack of a father is the one who is especially at risk. There is no doubt that in this country sheer economic pressure often precludes any realistic choice about the child's upbringing, and compels many mothers to offer their babies for adoption. This is bad enough, but the harm done is infinitely worse when the mother makes an unsuccessful attempt to keep her baby and later has to admit failure. In the intervening period the child has probably had several changes of home and a number of different people 'minding' him while his mother is at work.

Many others are like Veronica, who received no casework help of any kind when Alec was born. Hence she had no affiliation order for him, and for ten years she kept a household of three on what she earned as a typist and her mother's pension. Then came a financial crisis which she could not meet: Alec was to go to the Grammar School and the grant would not cover all the clothes he needed, and his bed had to be replaced as well. Her payments to the clothing club were already in arrears. She came to the agency's office, a tiny shabbily dressed woman who was almost speechless with embarrassment at having to ask for help, bringing all the accounts which had worried her for years. She refused to accept anything more than the grant which was quite easily obtained for her, although neither she nor Alec had ever had a holiday and there were no luxuries of any kind in her home. To be relieved of debt was all that she asked. It would have been impertinent and perhaps dangerous to persist in offering more, for all her energies were directed towards 'managing', and manage she must.

It is time we discarded from our public policy the last traces of the idea that an out-of-wedlock child is himself inferior, and that he must be placed at a disadvantage to expiate the sins of his parents. Certain legal and economic changes would do much to reduce the illegitimate child's personal and social handicap.

What can be done?

I. THE CHILD'S LEGAL STATUS

The law should recognise that every child has a father. To be told that he has no father is bewildering to a child because it raises doubts about his identity, and the fact is shameful to an adult because it embodies his illegitimate status. The slur of bastardy has a long history. In the Middle Ages a person born out of wedlock was 'nobody's child', and it was not until the Poor Law Act of 1844 was passed that his mother was recognised; she was given the right to apply to the court for an affiliation order for a sum not exceeding half-a-crown a week. An affiliation order, however, still does not imply any recognition of paternity, and although the father's name can appear on the birth certificate if he is present in person to register the birth, this also is no legal acknowledgment of his relationship to the child. Until very recently the father had no legal rights over his child, and no responsibilities except that of maintenance under an affiliation order. The law is, however, slowly moving in step with public opinion. The Adoption Act of 1958 gave the unmarried father the right to make representations about adoption arrangements, although his actual consent is still not required unless his name appears on the child's birth certificate. The Legitimacy Act of 1959 granted him the right to custody and access, and also allowed him to be regarded as the lawful father for guardianship purposes.

The logical next step in acknowledging the child's right to a father is to make provision for the father voluntarily to 'recognise' the child as his own, as was suggested in the pamphlet *Fatherless by Law?* published by the Church Assembly Board for Social Responsibility in 1966. This would not legitimise the child, but would legally establish a personal relationship between him and his father. A number of European countries have already adopted this procedure in varying forms; in general the child receives the right to inherit from his father and his family, as well as the same right to maintenance as the legitimate child enjoys. The recognition could be made by declaration, and alternatively it should be possible to insert the father's name on the birth certificate if an affiliation order is made against him, this amounting to an acknowledgment of paternity.

Secondly, it is desirable that the illegitimate child should be enabled to inherit from the relatives of both his parents on intestacy as though he were legitimate. At present he cannot do so unless he is mentioned by name in the will, and neither can he inherit on his mother's intestacy if she had legitimate children. This also should be changed, perhaps by an amendment to the Family Inheritance (Provisions) Act, 1938, whereby the Court would be enabled to make provision for him from the estate of either parent as though he were legitimate.*

Another much-needed reform is the complete removal from the law of the concept of parental 'possession' of a child. The principle that the child's welfare must be the first consideration in every decision concerning him seems to have been first stated in the Guardianship of Infants Act, 1886, and has often been reiterated since then, notably in the subsequent Act of 1925 and mainly in connection with custody proceedings in divorce, but the idea that a child 'belongs' to his parents as though he were a piece of property still lingers, and can operate very much against his best interests. Until recently it was necessary to prove a quite considerable degree of physical neglect or ill-treatment before the parental 'rights' could be overruled, but the 1958 Adoption Act's introduction of 'persistent failure to discharge the obligations of a parent' as grounds for dispensing with consent was a step in the right direction. Case law is still in process of determining the exact implications of the right to apply for custody conferred on the putative father by the Legitimacy Act, 1959, but the paramount importance of the child's wellbeing is slowly becoming established. Social workers, however, are still troubled by the fact that it is possible for neurotic or irresponsible parents to use the child as a pawn in a private game of their own, refusing to offer him for adoption or otherwise provide a stable home, and there is no legal sanction to prevent this even though the child may be gravely damaged; here the parental right to possession of the child still comes first.

A further reform that could well be considered has an indirect

* Legislation on these lines is included in the Family Law Reform Bill (December, 1968).

bearing on the illegitimate child's relationship with his parents. This is that it should be possible in England, as it has been in Scotland for some time, for a child who has been adopted to obtain from the Registrar General, after he has attained maturity, the name and address of his natural mother and of his father also if this is known. Social workers who have for long been accustomed to the 'clean break' theory in adoption practice may be sceptical about this, but research such as Alexina McWhinnie's[5] confirms that many adopted adolescents feel a great need to know who their parents were and where they were born, in order to establish their own identity. It does not necessarily follow that they will wish to get in touch with their biological parents, and experience in Scotland has not shown that any great difficulties are likely to arise. There is an increasing feeling that knowledge of one's origins is a basic human right which should not be denied to adopted persons who desire it.

2. FINANCIAL PROVISIONS

The three main resources for the maintenance of the unmarried mother and her child are, first, her own earnings, secondly, contributions from the putative father, and finally Social Security benefits. All of these have deficiencies which could be fairly easily remedied. With regard to affiliation orders, several changes are desirable. In the first place, it is to be hoped that if Family Courts are established in the future, all applications for maintenance will be transferred to them. The present system whereby the mother must wait her turn in the crowded anteroom of a Magistrates' Court causes her unnecessary distress, and deters many from applying at all. It seems likely that the maximum amount that can be awarded under an Order will shortly be raised to £5, but there is no reason why the law should specify any maximum sum at all; the criterion should surely be the standard of living that the child could reasonably expect if his parents were married.* It is desirable, too, that affiliation rights should be vested in the child himself, so that he is able to sue for maintenance through his 'best friend', that is, whoever has the care of him. At present only his mother can institute proceedings, and if she has disappeared or deserted him great hardship can be caused to his grandparents or other relatives. The local authority should also be able to take action on his behalf in this

* Legislation in 1968 has effected this change.

way. Again, the use of private agreements might well increase if they could be registered with the Court and payments made under them as with affiliation orders; this would make them at least as reliable as affiliation orders are at present.

The difficulty of enforcing payment on an Order, however, remains unaffected by these proposals, and uncertainty as to whether she will receive her money can cause great hardship to a mother. The Courts could well make greater use of their power to attach the man's earnings, or in other words to order that the stipulated sum should be deducted from his wages and paid directly to the Court by his employer. If she is drawing Supplementary Benefit the Commission is usually responsible for collecting affiliation payments, and the mother's basic allowance will be paid whether the father is contributing or not. This principle could well be extended to all maintenance payments for children in the form of an Unsupported Mother's Allowance payable through the Post Office. This would benefit divorced and deserted wives as well as unmarried mothers, and would alleviate much hardship. A statutory authority would be charged with the collection of the money due from the father, but the mother should receive her allowance whether he has paid it or not. In Denmark, where a similar scheme has been in operation for eighty years, it has been found that about 65 per cent of the fathers pay the required contribution.[6]

It would give the unmarried mother much greater economic stability if she could thus rely upon an adequate allowance from her child's father, guaranteed by the State. Her own earning capacity should also be improved if possible; Denmark has a special training scheme for unmarried mothers, which appears very successful.[7]

The proposed Unsupported Mother's Allowance would make by far the heaviest charge upon public funds; two other changes which are desirable would be less costly. One is that financial help should be available from the Supplementary Benefits Commission for pregnant girls under sixteen years old. It should be possible for the Commission to disregard the minimum age limit on production of a certificate of pregnancy, for many of these very young unmarried mothers come from disturbed home backgrounds where there may be no wage-earner to support them. The other point is that there is a need for greater flexibility in the amount and duration of grants paid by local authorities for the maintenance of residents in Mother and Baby Homes. The 'six weeks before and six weeks after confinement' rule does not meet every sort of circumstance; it is likely that if extra grants were more readily paid on behalf of those mothers who need residential care with their babies for several months, the extra cost would be offset by the saving effected by the growing number of girls who go straight home on discharge from hospital.

3. ACCOMMODATION

After finance, the greatest problem that faces many an unmarried mother who decides to keep her baby is to find somewhere to live. This is infinitely more difficult than if she were on her own, because it is closely tied up with the question of who will look after her child while she is at work. There is a great need for more self-contained flatlets with day nursery facilities at hand. The provision of this kind of accommodation is best effected by co-operation between statutory authorities and voluntary enterprise. Twenty or thirty schemes are already in existence, but there is room for many more. Details vary, but the aim is usually to offer to the more mature and capable girl a place where she can learn to be independent. Friendly help is available if she wants it, but she is not under supervision, and it is generally intended that after a year or two she will move to other quarters. The group is kept small, a large house being divided into about six or eight more or less self-contained units. Sometimes there is a day nursery close at hand, but if not, arrangements are usually made for the babies to be cared for, either on the premises or by approved 'minders', while their mothers are at work.

An even better solution to the problem of accommodation, however, is the kindly family who will receive an unmarried mother and her child as paying guests, and gradually absorb them into the household and the neighbourhood. People with the necessary qualities and qualifications are hard to find, and the 'matching' of landlady and lodgers must be skilfully done because the situation makes great demands on both sides, but success is well worth the effort involved because the girl and her child are integrated into the community and not segregated from it.

4. THE SOCIAL SERVICES

Is the present social service for unmarried parents adequate? There is universal agreement that it is not, but the grounds for criticism vary with the critic's standpoint. The secular-minded want the casework to be taken out of the hands of the churches, because they feel that even if it is no longer true to say that church workers are censorious or inclined to proselytise, nevertheless many clients are unwilling to approach a religious organisation for help. Church workers themselves are hampered by lack of resources and equipment, and many have overlarge caseloads. Yet there is to be found among them an amount of experience and skill which cannot at present be equalled among local authority workers dealing with the same problem.

The unmarried mother's need for a continuing relationship with the same caseworker from early pregnancy onwards has been one of the themes of this book. A unified social service for all unsupported mothers would certainly appear to be an effective way of ensuring that this relationship is available to them, and the Seebohm Report opens great opportunities for co-operation between the present voluntary and statutory agencies in providing such a service. Detailed arrangements will have to be worked out between the diocesan organisations on the one hand and the local authorities upon the other, but it is clear that each has much to contribute to a closer working partnership. Whatever form this may take in the future, the first consideration must always be 'What is best for the client?' Personal feelings, tradition and administrative difficulties can be left to come a long way after.

A unified social service will do a great deal to remove the stigma of illegitimacy, since it will be available to all divorced, deserted and separated wives as well as to unmarried women, and to all families unsupported for any reason. There will be need for more trained case-workers, including men, and it is possible that the service may develop on the lines already found in some Scandinavian countries. Every illegitimate child in Sweden has a *barnavardsman*, or child welfare guardian, who, although he is primarily responsible for the child's maintenance, nevertheless advises and assists the mother. In Denmark the Mothers' Aid organisation provides a comprehensive service, even to family counselling, home helps and holidays. In this country, apart from the need for continuous casework help, there is room for improvement in the adoption service. The practice of many agencies lags behind even such theoretical knowledge as we have, and in particular the procedure with regard to the mother's giving of her consent, and also the duties of the guardian *ad litem* are due for overhaul. Great efforts are also needed, perhaps on a national scale, to recruit new foster-parents and foster-'aunts' who will receive a pregnant girl or a mother with her baby, and also to give them adequate preparation for, and support in, the skilled and responsible work that they do.

We need a great deal more research into what actually happens to unmarried parents and their children, whether adopted or not; and more especially, research that will help with the most difficult question of all: when, and how best, to transplant a baby from one family to another.

Caseworkers are the backbone of any social service, but they do not effectively fulfil their function if their attention is directed too exclusively towards their clients' personal problems. It is understandable if a worker with an exacting caseload finds that it takes all her time and energies to cope with Grace and Helen and little Tommy, but nevertheless her responsibility does not end there. Indeed she cannot help them effectually unless she sees them in the round, and she is bound to be conscious of the effect on them of their social environment. She may be strongly aware, for example, that Helen's Supplementary Benefit is grossly inadequate for her needs, or that there is no special school available of the kind that Tommy requires. It may then be her duty to press those in authority for better social provisions. Again, she is a representative of an agency with a defined purpose; in her work she interprets and carries out its policy, but she must also be responsible for helping to formulate that policy. She will do this by participating in staff meetings and committee meetings, and by passing back the information she gains from her daily contact with her clients. How else can the administrators really know what they are doing? The four-hour-long ordeal of waiting for her turn in the Magistrates' Court for an affiliation application to be heard, and the mother's anguish at being questioned all over again by the guardian *ad litem* at the very end of the adoption process, are miseries that could be avoided by comparatively small changes in procedure, and the social worker who cares for her clients will be articulate in protest. She cannot simply contract out of her responsibility, nor refuse to be concerned with administrative and political solutions of her clients' problems. She will speak out for her clients in her agency, in her professional organisation, and in the promotion of new projects such as a local housing association for unsupported mothers. For she understands better than most people what awaits the girl without a wedding-ring who is going to have a baby.

Notes and References

1. *The Unmarried Mother*

1. Quoted from Nicholls and Wray, 'The History of the Foundling Hospital', in Hall and Howes, *The Church in Social Work*, p. 13.
2. R. W. Roberts, *The Unwed Mother*, p. 4.
3. *Registrar General's Statistical Review for England and Wales*, 1966.
4. J. Bowlby, *Child Care and the Growth of Love*, 2nd ed., p. 112.
5. See V. Wimperis, *The Unmarried Mother and Her Child*, p. 98.
6. D. Gough, 'Work with Unmarried Mothers', *The Almoner*, March, 1961.
7. B. Thompson, 'Social Study of Illegitimate Maternities', *British Journal of Social and Preventive Medicine*, April, 1956.
8. C. Greenland, 'Unmarried Parenthood', *The Medical Officer*, Vol. XCIX, January–June, 1958.
9. N. Pharaoh, 'Escape into Pregnancy', *New Society*, 19th September 1968.
10. Quoted in R. W. Roberts, *The Unwed Mother*, p. 247.
11. L. Young, *Out of Wedlock*, p. 41.
12. Ibid, pp. 36, 37.
13. Wimperis, op. cit., p. 97.
14. *The Guardian*, 11th October 1967.
15. M. Schofield, *Sexual Behaviour of Young People*, p. 122.
16. *Towards a Quaker View of Sex*, p. 45.
17. *Punch*, 12th July 1967.
18. An American scientist, Cattell, quoted in *The Unwed Mother*, reported that of fifty-four pregnant unmarried mothers he examined, thirty had character disorders, seven were neurotic and the remaining seventeen were schizophrenics. Not one was classified as normal.
19. R. Bernstein, quoted in *The Unwed Mother*, p. 110.

2. *The Individual and her Situation*

1. Jane Rowe, *Parents, Children and Adoption*, p. 10.
2. Ibid, p. 18.
3. M. A. Yelloly, 'Factors Relating to an Adoption Decision by the Mothers of Illegitimate Infants', *Sociological Review*, Vol. 13, No. 1, March 1965.

3. *The Unmarried Father*

1. F. Smith, 'The Young Unmarried Father', in *Pregnancy in Adolescence*: Report of a Conference sponsored by the National Council for the Unmarried Mother and Her Child, 1966.
2. L. Young, *Out of Wedlock*, p. 133.
3. See *News of the World*, 12th and 19th November 1967.
4. In Great Britain, see C. Greenland, 'Unmarried Parenthood: Putative Fathers', *Medical Officer*, 16th May 1958. In America see R. Pannor and M. Rowan, 'Work with Teen-age Unwed Parents and Their Families', *Child Welfare*, March 1961.
5. J. Bowlby, *Child Care and the Growth of Love*, 2nd ed., p. 114.
6. V. Wimperis, *The Unmarried Mother and Her Child*, p. 108.
7. L. Young, op. cit., p. 131.
8. M. Yelloly, *Social Casework with Unmarried Parents*, unpublished thesis, Liverpool University, 1964.
9. V. Wimperis, op. cit., p. 65.
10. F. Smith, op. cit.

4. *The Social Worker*

1. V. Wimperis, *The Unmarried Mother and Her Child*, p. 68.
2. I. Goodacre, *Adoption Policy and Practice*.
3. H. H. Perlman, *Social Casework*, p. 81.
4. M. L. Ferard and N. K. Hunnybun, *The Caseworker's Use of Relationships*, p. 48.
5. H. A. Williams, *The True Wilderness*, p. 102.
6. F. P. Biestek, *The Casework Relationship*, p. 3.
7. T. Douglas, 'Ethics in Social Work', *Case Conference*, July 1967.
8. G. Hamilton, *Theory and Practice of Social Casework*, 2nd ed., p. 121.
9. N. Timms, *Social Casework Principles and Practice*, p. 9.
10. J. Rowe, op. cit., p. 36.
11. A. McWhinnie, *Adoption Assessments*, p. 4.
12. G. Hamilton, op. cit., p. 121.
13. *Report of the Committee on Local Authority and Allied Personal Social Services*. Cmnd. 3703. H.M.S.O. 1968. Paragraph 211.

5. *The First Interview*

I am greatly indebted to the authors of the books on casework theory listed in the Bibliography. References in this chapter have been kept to a minimum, but many of the points raised are discussed in greater detail in the books mentioned, and a study of these is strongly recommended.

1. F. P. Biestek, *The Casework Relationship*, p. 80.

2. See especially Biestek, op. cit., p. 89, and N. Leighton, The Myth of Self-Determination', *New Society*, 23rd February 1967.

3. H. H. Perlman, *Social Casework*, p. 159.

6. *Coming to a Decision*

1. F. Hollis, *Casework: A Psychosocial Therapy*, p. 154.

2. P. Halmos, *The Faith of the Counsellors*, p. 156ff.

3. J. Rowe, *Parents, Children and Adoption*, p. 55.

4. M. Yelloly, *Social Casework with Unmarried Parents*, unpublished thesis, Liverpool University, 1964.

5. J. Rowe, op. cit., p. 49.

6. F. Hollis, op. cit., p. 95.

7. F. P. Biestek, *The Casework Relationship*, p. 110.

8. Welfare Council of Toronto, *Study of Illegitimacy*, 1943.

9. J. Rowe, op. cit., p. 271.

10. L. Young, *Out of Wedlock*, p. 187.

11. J. Bowlby, *Child Care and the Growth of Love*, 2nd ed., p. 119.

12. M. Yelloly, 'Factors Relating to an Adoption Decision by the Mothers of Illegitimate Infants', *Sociological Review*, Vol. 13, No. 1, 1965.

13. M. Yelloly, unpublished thesis.

14. M. Yelloly, 'Adoption and the Natural Mother', *Case Conference*, December 1966.

15. R. Bernstein, 'Are We Still Stereotyping the Unmarried Mother?' in *The Unwed Mother*, ed. R. W. Roberts, p. 113.

16. J. Bowlby, op. cit., p. 125. See also D. W. Winnicott, *The Child, The Family and The Outside World*, p. 55.

17. R. Bernstein, op. cit., p. 124.

7. *Adoption: Casework with the Mother*

1. M. Yelloly, 'Factors Relating to an Adoption Decision by the Mothers of Illegitimate Infants', *Sociological Review*, Vol. 13, No. 1, March 1965.

2. See J. Rowe, *Parents, Children and Adoption*, Chapter 7, Also A. Colville, 'Adoption for the Handicapped Child', and R. Taft, 'Adoptive Families for "Unadoptable" Children', in *Readings in Adoption*, ed. by I. Evelyn Smith.

3. J. Bowlby, *Child Care and the Growth of Love*, 2nd ed., p. 124.

4. For fuller discussion of foster-homes, see: J. Bowlby, op. cit., Chapter 12. Also B. Smith, 'Finding Foster-homes for Pre-adoption Babies', *Case Conference*, November 1966, and N. Kay, 'Foster Parents as Resources', *Case Conference*, October 1967.

5. See N. Autton, *The Pastoral Care of the Bereaved*, S.P.C.K., 1966.

6. See E. Younghusband, 'Adoption and the Unmarried Mother', in *Social Work and Social Change.*

7. See V. Wimperis, *The Unmarried Mother and Her Child*, p. 107. Also Hollis, Bowlby, Young, op. cit.

8. *Keeping the Baby*

1. R. Bernstein, 'Are We Still Stereotyping the Unmarried Mother?' in *The Unwed Mother*, ed. R. W. Roberts, p. 113.

2. See V. Wimperis, *The Unmarried Mother and Her Child*, p. 126.

3. For further discussion of available resources, see V. Wimperis, *The Unmarried Mother and Her Child*, Chapters 6 and 7.

4. E. Younghusband, *Social Work and Social Change*, p. 61.

9. *Looking to the Future*

1. Alexina McWhinnie, *Adopted Children: How They Grow Up*, 1967.

2. DEATHS OF INFANTS UNDER ONE YEAR OF AGE

Year	Deaths per 1000 of total live births	Deaths per 1000 legitimately born	Deaths per 1000 illegitimately born
1918	97	91	186
1936	59	57	88
1946	43	42	60
1956	24	23	29
1965	19	19	25

—*Registrar-General's Statistical Review of England and Wales*

3. E. Younghusband, *Social Work and Social Change*, p. 59.

4. P. Shapiro, 'Illegitimacy and Child Care', *New Society*, 18th January 1968.

5. A. McWhinnie, op. cit., p. 268. See also Church Assembly Board for Social Responsibility, *Fatherless by Law?*, p. 9.

6. National Council for the Unmarried Mother and Her Child, *Social Provision for the Illegitimate Child and His Mother*, p. 2.

7. V. Skalts and M. Norgaard, *Mothers' Aid in Denmark*, p. 12.

Bibliography

Social Casework Theory and Practice

Association of Social Workers: *New Thinking for Changing Needs* (London 1963).

Biestek, Felix P.: *The Casework Relationship* (George Allen & Unwin, London 1961).

Ferard, Margaret L., and Hunnybun, Noel K.: *The Caseworker's Use of Relationships* (Tavistock Publications, London 1962).

Garrett, Annette: *Interviewing: Its Principles and Methods* (Family Service Association of America, New York 1942).

Halmos, Paul: *The Faith of the Counsellors* (Constable, London 1965).

Hamilton, Gordon: *Theory and Practice of Social Casework*, 2nd edition (Columbia University Press, New York 1951).

Heywood, Jean: *Casework and Pastoral Care* (S.P.C.K., London 1967).

Hollis, Florence: *Casework: A Psychosocial Therapy* (Random House, New York 1964).

Leighton, N.: 'The Myth of Self-Determination, *New Society*, 23rd February 1967.

Perlman, Helen Harris: *Social Casework: A Problem-Solving Process* (University of Chicago Press 1957).

Timms, Noel: *Social Casework* (Routledge & Kegan Paul Ltd., London 1964).

Winnicott, Clare: *Child Care and Social Work* (Codicote Press, Welwyn 1964).

Younghusband, Eileen: *Social Work and Social Change* (George Allen & Unwin, London 1964).

Ethics and Morality

British Council of Churches: *Sex and Morality* (1966).

Demant, V. A.: *An Exposition of Christian Sex Ethics* (Hodder & Stoughton, London 1963).

Friends' Home Service Committee: *Towards a Quaker View of Sex* (1963).

Hodgson, Leonard: *Sex and Christian Freedom* (S.C.M. Press, London 1967).

Keeling, Michael: *Morals in a Free Society* (S.C.M. Press, London 1967).

Williams, H. A.: *The True Wilderness* (Constable, London 1965).

Unmarried Parenthood and Illegitimacy

Bowlby, John: *Child Care and the Growth of Love*, 2nd edition (Pelican, Harmondsworth 1963).

Church Assembly Board for Social Responsibility: *Fatherless by Law?* (1966).

Fletcher, Ronald: *The Family and Marriage* (Penguin, Harmondsworth 1962).

Goodacre, Iris: *Adoption Policy and Practice* (George Allen & Unwin, London 1966).

Gough, Donald: *Understanding Unmarried Mothers* (National Council for the Unmarried Mother and Her Child, London 1966).

Greenland, Cyril: 'Unmarried Parenthood', *The Medical Officer*, Vol. XCIX, January–June 1958.

Greenland, Cyril: 'Unmarried Parenthood: Putative Fathers', *The Medical Officer*, 10 May 1958.

Hall, M. Penelope and Howes, Ismene V.: *The Church Social Work* (Routledge and Kegan Paul, London 1965).

Kay, N.: 'Foster Parents as Resources', *Case Conference*, October 1967.

McWhinnie, Alexina: *Adopted Children: How They Grow Up* (Routledge & Kegan Paul, London 1967).

McWhinnie, Alexina: *Adoption Assessments* (Standing Conference of Societies Registered for Adoption, London 1966).

National Council for the Unmarried Mother and Her Child: *Affiliation Proceedings in English or Welsh Courts* (1960).

National Council for the Unmarried Mother and Her Child: *Social Provision for the Illegitimate Child and His Mother* (1966).

Pannor, R. and Rowan, M.: 'Work with Teen-age Unmarried Parents and Their Families', *Child Welfare*, December 1959; 'An assertive Casework Approach to the Older Unmarried Father', *Child Welfare*, March 1961.

Roberts, Robert W. (ed.): *The Unwed Mother* (Harper & Row, New York 1966).

Rowe, Jane: *Parents, Children and Adoption* (Routledge & Kegan Paul, London 1966).

Schofield, Michael: *The Sexual Behaviour of Young People* (Longmans, Green & Co Ltd London 1965).

Shapiro, P.: 'Illegitimacy and Child Care', *New Society*, 18th January 1968.

Skalts, V. and Norgaard, M.: *Mothers' Aid in Denmark* (Det Danske Selskab, Copenhagen 1965).

Smith, B.: 'Finding Foster-homes for Pre-Adoption Babies', *Case Conference*, November 1966.

Smith, I. Evelyn (ed.): *Readings in Adoption* (Philosophical Library, New York 1963).
Thompson, B.: 'Social Study of Illegitimate Maternities', *British Journal of Social and Preventive Medicine*, April 1956.
Welfare Council of Toronto: *A Study of Unmarried Mothers and Their Children* (1943).
Wilkinson, G. S.: *Legal Aspects of Illegitimacy* (National Council for the Unmarried Mother and Her child, London 1965).
Wimperis, Virginia: *The Unmarried Mother and Her Child* (George Allen & Unwin, London 1960).
Winnicott, D. W.: *The Child, The Family and the Outside World* (Pelican, Harmondsworth 1964).
Yelloly, M. A.: *Social Casework with Unmarried Parents* (Unpublished Thesis, Liverpool University 1964).
Yelloly, M. A.: 'Factors Relating to an Adoption Decision by the Mothers of Illegitimate Infants', *Sociological Review*, Vol. 13, No. 1, March 1965.
Young, Leontine: *Out of Wedlock* (McGraw-Hill, New York 1964).

Fiction

Banks, Lynne Reid: *The L-shaped Room* (Penguin, Harmondsworth 1962).
Barstow, Stan: *A Kind of Loving* (Penguin, Harmondsworth 1962).
Hawthorne, Nathaniel: *The Scarlet Letter* (Signet, New York 1959).

The Ethics and Morality and the Fiction sections of the above list are small and arbitrary selections from the vast number of books on these subjects.

Index